EDITOR: MARTIN WINDROW

OSPREY
MILITARY

MEN-AT-AR

THE FRENC
THE AMERICAN
OF INDEPENDENCE

Text by
RENÉ CHARTRAND
Colour plates by
FRANCIS BACK

Published in 1991 by
Osprey Publishing Ltd
59 Grosvenor Street, London W1X 9DA
© Copyright 1991 Osprey Publishing Ltd

ISBN 1 83332 167 X

Filmset in Great Britain
Printed through Bookbuilders Ltd, Hong Kong

For a catalogue of all books published by Osprey Military
please write to:

The Marketing Manager,
Consumer Catalogue Department,
Osprey Publishing Ltd,
Michelin House, 81 Fulham Road,
London SW3 6RB

Dedication
The author and the artist wish to dedicate this book to
our long-time friends, Mr. & Mrs. Eugène Lelièpvre.

Acknowledgements

We gratefully acknowledge the assistance given by
Albert W. Haarmann, Arwed Ulrich Koch, Eugène
Lelièpvre, Michel Pétard, Jean Boudriot, Marko
Zlatich, Raoul Brunon, the Musée de l'Armée at Paris
and at Salon-de-Provence, the Archives Nationales
and La Sabretache in Paris, the Rochefort Archives,
the National Archives of Canada, the Royal Canadian
Military Institute Library, the University of Ottawa
Library, the National Library of Canada, the
Canadian Park Service Library, the Library of
Congress, and especially the Anne S. K. Brown
Military Collection at Brown University (USA).

Author's note
The American War of Independence was one of the
finest hours for France's military and naval forces and
certainly the best during the 18th century. At last,
France managed to humble her ancient enemy in 1783
just as she had been humbled twenty years earlier.
Wars are not usually won by accident, and this short
study looks at the transformations which occurred in
the French armies and navy from 1763. Today, we
usually think of Count Rochambeau's army in the
United States as France's most important contribution
to the war. Is this a correct impression? How
important were the troop movements in other theatres,
and what were the obscure colonial troops one comes
across from time to time? Our study will also attempt
to answer these questions and give a global view of the
French armed forces deployed around the world
during this struggle.

The historic French or Spanish names have been
kept in most cases. Saint-Domingue (called 'San
Domingo' by anglophone authors) is now Haiti, Île-
de-France is Mauritius, Île-de-Bourbon is La
Réunion, the Dutch East Indies are Indonesia, Ceylon
is Sri Lanka.

CHRONOLOGY

This chronology of battles is not exhaustive but will guide the reader as to most engagements in the various parts of the globe. We have added the names of participating French units, but the reader should not consider our listing definitive, especially with regards to naval battles.

1778

27 July: Naval battle of Ushant, off France. *Bombardiers de la Marine*, *Corps royal d'infanterie de la Marine*. Detachments of troops serving as marines on French fleet from Regts. Normandie, Auvergne, Dauphin, Condé.

7 September: French capture Dominica. 1,800 troops from Regts. Auxerrois, Viennois (grenadiers & chasseurs), Martinique (grenadiers & chasseurs); *Cadet de Saint-Pierre* company, Martinique militia.

14 September: British capture Saint-Pierre-et-Miquelon. *Compagnie franche de Saint-Pierre-et-Miquelon*.

17 October: British capture Pondichery, India. Regt. Pondichery, *Canonnier-Bombardiers de l'Inde*, Sepoys, militia.

13 December: British capture St. Lucia. 80 men of Regt. Martinique, 16 gunners of *Royal-Artillerie*, militia. French counter-attack 18 December with troops from Regts. Armagnac, Martinique, Guadeloupe and militia, but repulsed by British.

1779

31 January: French capture Saint-Louis, Senegal.

Detachments of Regts. La Reine, Languedoc, Forèz, Walsh, 2nd Legion *Volontaires étrangers de la Marine*.

1 May: Unsuccessful French raid on Jersey, Channel Islands. *Volontaires de Nassau*.

18 June: French capture St. Vincent. 200 troops from Regts. Champagne, Viennois, Martinique, *Canonniers-bombardiers des Îles-du-Vent*, 200 Martinique militia volunteers, joined by 600 Caribs.

4 July: French capture Grenada. 1,700 troops from Regts. Dillon, det. of Auxerrois, Martinique, Cambresis, Foix, 1st Legion *Volontaires étrangers de la Marine*, Viennois (grenadiers), Hainault (grenadiers), Champagne (chasseurs), artillery.

13 September–18 October: Unsuccessful Franco-American siege of Savannah (Georgia). 2,800 French troops detached from Regts. Armagnac, Auxerrois, Agenois, Cambresis, Champagne, Dillon, Gatinois, Hainault, Foix, Walsh, Royal-Artillerie, Du Cap, Port-au-Prince, Guadeloupe & Martinique, 156 *Grenadiers volontaires de Saint-Domingue*, 545 *Chasseurs volontaires de Saint-Domingue*, detachments of Condé and Belsunce Dragoon Regts., *Canonniers-bombardiers de Saint-Domingue*.

23 September: Naval battle off Flamborough Head, UK, mainly between the American ship *Bonhomme Richard* and HMS *Serapis*. A detachment of about 140 men from the Walsh regiment served as marines on board Captain John Paul Jones' American ship.

1780

21 February–12 May: British siege and capture of Charleston, South Carolina. A detachment of *Grenadiers volontaires de Saint-Domingue* serves with the American garrison.

17 April, 15 & 19 May: Naval battles off Martinique. *Bombardiers de la Marine*, *Corps royal d'infanterie de la Marine*. Detachments of troops serving as marines on French fleet from Regts.

3

Armagnac, Champagne, Auxerrois, Viennois, Touraine, La Sarre, Brie, Poitou, Dillon, Walsh, Enghien, Martinique, 1st Legion *Volontaires étrangers de la Marine*, *Volontaires de Bouillé*, *Canonniers-bombardiers des Îles-du-Vent*.

17–18 December: French repulse British attack on St. Vincent. 800 troops from Regts. Auxerrois, Viennois, 300 militia and Caribs.

1781

5 January: Unsuccessful French attack on Jersey, Channel Islands. Volontaires de Luxembourg.

February: British capture Dutch West Indian islands of St. Martin, Saba and St. Eustatius. The Dutch colonies of Demerara, Essequibo and Berbice in South America, Trincomalee in Ceylon and Negapatan in India also fell to the British this year.

16 April: Naval battle of Porto Praya, Cape Verde islands. *Bombardiers de la Marine, Corps royal d'infanterie de la Marine*. Detachments of troops serving as marines on French fleet from Regt. Austrasie.

10–12 May: French raid on St. Lucia. This was a feint for the attack on Tobago (see below for troops involved).

26 May: Siege and capture of Pensacola (Florida) by Spanish. French detachment of 800 also present from Regts. Poitou, Agenois (including chasseurs), Gatinois, Cambresis, Du Cap.

4 June: French capture Tobago. 2,500 troops from Regts. Viennois, Brie, Dillon, grenadiers & chasseurs of Armagnac and Auxerrois; chasseurs of Walsh and Royal-Comtois.

12 July: French raid on the Tory fort at Lloyd Neck, Long Island, NY (USA). Detachment of 200 men from Regts. Bourbonnois, Royal Deux-Ponts, Soissonnois, Saintonge.

5 September: Naval battle of Chesapeake Bay. *Bombardiers de la Marine, Corps royal d'infanterie de la Marine*. Detachments of troops serving as marines on French fleet from Regts. La Sarre, Brie.

28 September–19 October: Franco-American siege and capture of Yorktown (Virginia). Regts. Bourbonnois, Royal Deux-Ponts, Soissonnois,

Naval battle on 18 December 1779 between the French and British fleets within view of Fort Royal, Martinique. To the left, French ships flying the plain white standard – the flag used on ships of war and forts until the advent of the tricolour in 1790 – sail out. In the foreground are the batteries of Fort Royal crowded with military personnel and civilians looking at the battle. The gunners of the Canonniers-bombardiers are seen preparing canons and mortars for action. They wear a practical undress uniform consisting of a blue forage cap with red trim, blue jacket with red collar and cuffs, white breeches and black gaiters. Engraving after a painting in the Musée de la Marine in Paris.

Saintonge, Agenois, Gatinois, Touraine, Royal-Artillerie, Légion de Lauzun, 1st Legion *Volontaires étranger de la Marine* (hussars only), *Corps royal d'infanterie de la Marine*.

26 November: French capture St. Eustatius. 1,500 troops from Regts. Auxerrois, Royal-Comtois, Dillon, Walsh. As a result, St. Martin & Saba also surrender.

1782

6 January–5 February: Siege and capture of Fort St. Philip at Mahon, Minorca, by Spanish and French. 4,000 troops from Regts. Royal-Suedois, Bretagne, Lyonnois, Bouillon, Royal-Artillerie joined the Spanish forces.

30 January: French capture Demerara. Detachments from Regt. Armagnac, 335 men from 1st Legion *Volontaires étranger de la Marine*, (probably) *Troupes nationales de Cayenne*. As a result, Essequebo and Berbice also surrender on 1 & 5 February.

13 February: French capture St. Kitts. 6,000 troops from Regts. Armagnac, Agenois, Au-xerrois, Touraine, Viennois, Brie, Royal-Comtois, Dillon, 1st Legion *Volontaires étranger de la Marine* (hussars only), *Volontaires de Bouillé*; artillery.

18 February: Naval battle off Madras, India. *Bombardiers de la Marine, Corps royal d'infanterie de la Marine*. Detachments of troops serving as marines on French fleet from 3rd Legion *Volontaires étranger de la Marine, Volontaires de Bourbon*.

20 February: French capture Nevis.

22 February: French capture Montserrat. 500 men from Regt. Auxerrois.

12 April: Naval battle of the Saints. *Bombardiers de la Marine, Corps royal d'infanterie de la Marine*. Detachments of troops serving as marines on French fleet from Regts. Armagnac, Champagne, Auxerrois, Agenois, Gatinois, Touraine, Beauce, Viennois, Monsieur, Foix, Dillon, *Canonniers-bombardiers des Îles-du-Vent*.

6 July: Naval battle off Negapatan, India. *Bombardiers de la Marine, Corps royal d'infanterie de la Marine*. Detachments of troops serving as marines on French fleet from Regts. Îsle-de-France, Austrasie, 3rd Legion *Volontaires étranger de la Marine*, *Volontaires de Bourbon*.

July 1782–March 1783: Unsuccessful siege and blockade of Gibraltar by Spanish and French. 4,000 French troops from Regts. Royal-Suedois, Bretagne, Lyonnois, Bouillon, Royal-Artillerie joined the Spanish forces.

25–30 August: French siege and capture of Trincomalee, Ceylon. 1,850 troops detached from Regts. Îsle-de-France, Austrasie, 3rd Legion *Volontaires étrangers de la Marine*, *Volontaires de Bourbon*, *Bombardiers de la Marine*, *Corps royal d'infanterie de la Marine*, Royal-Artillerie with 700 Sepoys and 100 Malays (native troops from the Dutch East Indies).

8–31 August: French capture and destroy Fort Prince of Wales, York Factory and Severn in Hudson's Bay, Canada. 250 man det. of Regts. Armagnac, Auxerrois; *Canonniers-bombardiers de Saint-Domingue, Corps royal d'infanterie de la Marine*.

1783

March–July: French corps of 2 Bns. of Regt. Îsle-de-France and artillery campaigns with Tipoo Sultan's army in southern India on Malabar coast. Participates in the capture of Voloze, Bednor (3 May), Onor, siege of Mangalore from 6 May to July.

20 June: Naval battle off Cuddelore, India. *Bombar-diers de la Marine, Corps royal d'infanterie de la Marine*. Detachments of troops serving as marines on French fleet from Regts. Forèz, Austrasie, Royal-Artillerie, Sepoys.

13–29 June: French defence of Cuddelore, India. Regts. Austrasie, La Mark, Royal-Roussillon, Aquitaine, Royal-Artillerie, Îsle-de-France, 1st Legion *Volontaires étranger de la Marine*, *Volontaires de Bourbon*, Sepoy battalions.

THE LEGACY OF THE SEVEN YEARS' WAR

The French forces which fought during the American War of Independence were, to a very large extent, a product of the disasters that the Seven Years' War (1756–1763) brought to the armies of France. During that war, just about everything that could have gone wrong did so: the fleet had been swept off the oceans, especially after Quiberon in 1759—the 'Year of Victories' for the British—and nearly all colonies had been lost. In Europe, the war had started off fairly well with the capture of Minorca and some minor successes in Germany. Then came a series of disastrous defeats to the combined forces of

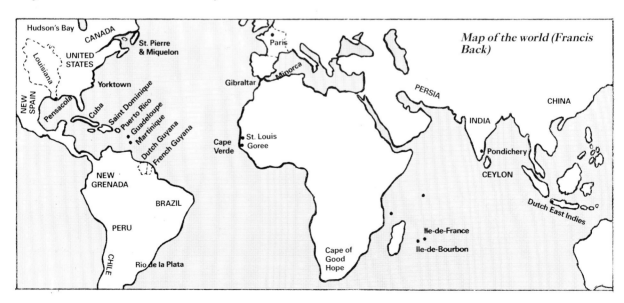

Map of the world (Francis Back)

France, Austria and Russia, struck by the military genius of Frederick the Great of Prussia and his army. By 1762, fellow Bourbon King Carlos III of Spain tried to rescue his French cousin Louis XV only to see his colonial capitals of Havana and Manila fall to the British. The Treaty of Paris in 1763 confirmed the loss of North America, of India (except for a few posts), of valuable West Indian islands, of most of Senegal, and humiliating clauses such as the destruction of the fortifications of Dunkirk.

Well before the end of the war, the court of France was getting desperate; a rapid succession of ministers were briefly responsible for the army and the navy. There was increasing discontent among the French public and, at the news of defeat after defeat, sweeping reforms were demanded. The man who initiated these reforms was the Duke of Choiseul, a man of considerable ability and tenacity who had been foreign minister until 1761. By then it was obvious that the war was lost, and he was appointed by the king to be minister of both the army and the navy—all military forces on land and sea. Choiseul inherited a demoralised army still basically functioning as in the days of Louis XIV.[1] As late as the 1740s, Marshal De Saxe was writing of his 'dreams' that it should one day march in step! The fleet was all but lost and equally disgraced—'a corps which must be totally reformed if it is to be of any use', the Duke d'Aiguillon wrote sternly. However, public pressure and the humiliations to France's glory gave Choiseul more liberty than had been the case for some of his predecessors, who had been fighting strongly held vested interests.

Reforms in the Army

Choiseul went to work with determination, making sure that he made himself available for a suitable number of consultations—including putting up with a review board of some eighty generals. From the end of 1762 a series of royal orders dictated by common sense and good planning were signed by the king, and a vast reorganisation was started. From then on, regiments would all be organised the same way, have the same training, be supplied by the Crown, and attend large summer training camps for brigade and division manoeuvres. Weapons were improved, and

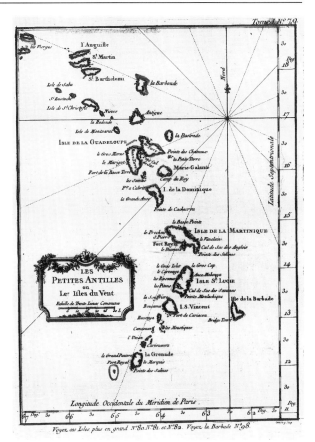

Map of the Leeward and smaller Windward islands in the West Indies. This area saw considerable fighting between 1778 and 1782, most British islands being captured by the French. (National Archives of Canada, NMC 15883)

uniforms standardised down to stamping the regiment's number on the buttons. Regimental officers were held accountable at their various levels, thus abolishing the percentage system on clothing and other items; recruiting was centralised, abolishing yet another officer's 'perk'. All this was not achieved without grumbling from the officer corps, but within a couple of years the new ways were accepted. Riding schools were established for the cavalry, and from 1765 the artillery system devised by General Gribeauval was adopted. For all his good sense and sound reforms Choiseul made many enemies at court; he managed to elude them until 1771 when the devious courtesan Madame du Barry finally convinced an aged Louis XV, no doubt in the comfort of his bed, that Choiseul had to go.

By then, however, the work of the skilled minister had convinced many; and Choiseul's successors

[1] See our MAA 203 Louis XIV's Army.

followed his course of reforms in spite of accusations of 'Prussianising' the army. Of these, the Count de Saint-Germain, minister from 1775, caused the most uproar by trying to introduce corporal punishment, abolishing part of the King's Guards including the Musketeers and the Horse Grenadiers as too expensive, abolishing the purchase system for officers' commissions, and retiring some of the 865 colonels. He reorganised, mainly for the better, everything from the supply system to the militia, and introduced a rather strange infantry uniform in 1776 (which we will see in detail later). Louis XVI, king since 10 May 1774, supported his minister; but while most of Saint-Germain's reforms are now seen as good, the

controversies in his own day were such that he resigned in 1777. The Prince de Montbarrey, a smoother courtier, carried on until 1780, and Marshal de Ségur until 1787. It was during Ségur's ministry that the infamous royal order of 22 May 1781 was issued, requiring henceforth that only noblemen would qualify for officers' commissions. Ségur was against it, but had to comply with the wishes of the king's brother (the future Louis XVIII) and his clique. Cruelly ironic, considering that the French army was then fighting for the liberty of Americans, the order was bitterly resented by talented NCOs and enlisted men, who did not forget this injustice when their hour came eight years later.

From 25 March and 31 May 1776, all infantry regiments (except the Guards and the Régiment du Roi) were ordered to have two battalions. For the older four-battalion regiments this meant that their 2nd and 4th battalions became new regiments. The year before, several infantry battalions had been sent to the West Indies, and so the 4th Battalion of La Marine became the 2nd of the new Regiment of Auxerrois; Navarre became Armagnac; Guyenne became Viennois; Béarn became Agenois; Auvergne became Gâtinois; and Flandres became Cambrésis. Previously, each battalion had nine companies, but Count Saint-Germain decreased the number of officers and added more enlisted men to each company. Battalions now had six companies: one of grenadiers, one of the newly created chasseurs, and four of fusiliers. An auxiliary recruit company was added in wartime. The strength was as follows:

Grenadier company: 1 captain, 1 second-captain, 1 first-lieutenant, 1 second-lieutenant, 2 sub-lieutenants, 1 sergeant-major, 1 *fourrier-écrivain* (roughly Q.M. sgt), 4 sergeants, 8 corporals, 1 gentleman-cadet, 1 *frater* (roughly a surgeon's assistant), 84 grenadiers and 2 drummers. Total: 108.

Chasseur and fusilier companies: 1 captain, 1 second-captain, 1 first-lieutenant, 1 second-lieutenant, 2 sub-lieutenants, 1 sergeant-major, 1 *fourrier-écrivain*, 5 sergeants, 10 corporals, 1 gentleman-cadet, 1 *frater* (roughly a surgeon's assistant), 144 chasseurs or fusiliers and 2 drummers. Total: 171.

Regimental staff: 1 colonel commanding, 1 second-colonel, 1 lieutenant-colonel, 1 major, 1 quarter-master treasurer, 2 ensigns, 1 adjutant, 1 surgeon-major, 1 chaplain, 1 drum-major and 1 armourer. Total: 12. The wartime Auxiliary company was the same as the chasseurs and fusiliers, but had no gentleman-cadet and the number of recruits was, of course, variable.

Thus, at peak strength, each battalion had 963 officers and men, plus 26 officers and other ranks attached to the auxiliary recruit company, plus the regimental 12 staff for an establishment of 1,990 all ranks for the two battalions of each regiment. Such a strong establishment was to be achieved gradually according to the March 1776 order. Initially, chasseur and fusilier companies were at 116 enlisted men, and it is reasonable to think that peak strength was not often reached, especially in units posted to the West or East Indies. For instance, during 1783 in India, the 2nd Battalion of La Mark only had 350 while the 2nd of Aquitaine had 600. The actual

Dress uniform of a Marèchal de camp (roughly, a brigadier) according to the 2 September 1775 dress regulation in force at the time of the American War of Independence. It is typical of the uniforms worn by French general officers and staff at the time and consisted of a completely blue coat with gold lace and buttons, scarlet waistcoat laced with gold and scarlet breeches. Photo by Raoul Brunon. (Bibliothèque Raoul & Jean Brunon, Musée de l'Armée, Château de l'Empéri, Salon-de-Provence, France)

Aide-de-Camps were required to wear a special uniform, as shown in this c. 1776 illustration, consisting of a completely dark blue coat with scarlet waistcoat and breeches, *gold buttons and lace. The horse furnishings were scarlet and gold. (Anne S. K. Brown Military Collection, Brown University, Providence, USA)*

average battalion strength was about 500, and this was the number used for the battalions sent to the United States and Minorca.

The French army's royal corps of artillery saw considerable reforms during this period which saw the introduction, against many objections, of the excellent Gribeauval system. From 1765, *Royal-Artillerie* was composed of 7 regiments, each with the name of its HQ location: La Fère, Metz, Strasbourg, Grenoble, Besançon, Auxonne, Toul. From 3 November 1776 each regiment had 20 companies (divided into two battalions of 10 companies, or into five brigades of 4 companies each) of which 4 were of bombardiers, 2 of sappers and the rest of gunners. All companies had 1 captain, 3 lieutenants and 71 NCOs and men. Not attached to the regiments were a further 6 companies of miners and 9 companies of *ouvriers* (pioneers) and a large body of officers attached to artillery research, design and manufacture supervision. The establishment totalled 909

officers and 11,805 men. It could be said that, at this period, the corps was probably the finest and most advanced artillery organisation existing.

By these various reforms, the establishment was brought up from 90,000 to nearly 170,000 infantry and from 25,000 to 46,000 cavalry at the eve of the war. To support the infantry and artillery even further, provincial militia battalions were ordered activated on 30 January 1778. From these 13 regiments of *Grenadiers royaux* were formed with the grenadier companies, 13 regiments attached to the 7 regular artillery regiments, 5 regiments attached to the engineers, and the Paris and Corsica provincial regiments for those areas. Some 79 battalions were each attached to a regular regiment to serve as a third battalion. These 75,000 embodied militiamen did garrison and coast guard duty in France during the war and all provided volunteer recruits to their regiment.

The French army that the British army would face from 1778 was completely different from that of 20 years earlier. By all accounts it was impeccably drilled, well armed, well equipped, capable of fearsome firepower, and led by a competent officer corps which had done a lot of hard work and study. Trained mainly to face the Prussian or Austrian armies in a continental war, it performed extremely well in the various overseas operations, usually holding the British forces at bay when not compelling the enemy to surrender. It could be added that the work of the staff officers and the engineers was disciplined and impressive, and that most general officers—men such as Count de Rochambeau and the Marquis de Bouillé—were of a bold, yet crisp and measured temper.

Reforms in the Navy

When Choiseul took the naval portfolio in 1761 there was hardly a navy left. The stores were empty, there was no money, the few ships of the line existing were abandoned in ports, sailors were scarce, officers were dispirited, and remnants of marines and colonial troops repatriated from fallen colonies hovered about the seaports. The duke incorporated the sea-soldiers into the line infantry at the end of 1761; then went to work on a naval programme assisted by Admiral Truguet which called for a fleet of 80 ships of the line and 47 frigates. Choiseul appealed to the public for money to help. The response from the humiliated nation, which sensed the importance of naval power, was enthusiastic. The province of Languedoc contributed first in 1762 to build an 80-gun ship, an example followed by Brittany, Burgundy, Artois, Flanders; by cities such as Bordeaux, Paris, Marseilles; and by groups of financiers and individual subscriptions sponsoring mostly 74-gun ships. While construction was under way, the first great naval regulation since 1689 was signed on 25 March 1765. Incapable officers were retired, training became a high priority, and naval artillery was improved. The navy became an independent ministry again in 1766. As in the army, the successors of Choiseul followed his lead, the most talented and energetic being Gabriel de Sartines, minister from 1774, and Marshal de Castries from 1780. By 1778 some 52 ships of the line were afloat, and this grew to 73 by 1782.

From late 1762 the duties of sea-soldiers were assigned to army regiments with debatable success; in 1769 some marine 'brigades' were raised, which became regiments in 1772, but the regimental organisation did not work too well. On 26 December 1774 de Sartines reorganised the whole force into 100 companies of a *Corps royal d'infanterie de la Marine*, and the élite artillerymen into 3 companies of *Bombardiers de la Marine*. It was an establishment of 12,248 officers and men, organised as follows:

Marine company: 1 naval lieutenant as captain, 2 naval ensigns as lieutenants, 1 *fourrier*, 6 sergeants, 6 corporals, 6 *appointés* (lance-corporals), 96 fusiliers, 3 drummers. Total: 121.

Bombardier company: 2 naval lieutenants as captain and second-captain, 2 naval ensigns as lieutenants, 1 *fourrier*, 2 sergeants, 4 corporals, 12 artificers, 50 bombardiers, 1 drummer. Total: 74.

These troops provided excellent services during the war; but there was a considerable shortage of marines which could only be compensated by using thousands of army soldiers—mostly volunteers—as marine detachments. There was a reorganisation with an increased establishment in 1782, but this does not seem to have been carried into effect before the end of hostilities. The navy also had a coast guard militia, which was reorganised on 13 December 1778 as independent companies of coast guard artillery which were partly activated during the war.

The reverses suffered by Great Britain during the

The officers in charge of army administration, finances and supplies such as this Commissaire ordinnateur *wore a grey coat with scarlet cuffs, turnbacks, waistcoat and breeches trimmed with* gold and buttons. They were part of the staff and present all fronts. (Anne S. K. Brown Military Collection, Brown University, Providence, USA)*

American War of Independence were directly related to the fact that the French navy managed to keep the Royal Navy at bay. The lines of communication with America and Asia were kept open, and the British put on the defensive. In this the French were helped by the Spanish from 1779, and the Dutch to a lesser extent from 1780. But without the French navy the chances of success against the world's most powerful fleet were unthinkable. French admirals did fairly well on the whole—Admiral de Grasse's victory at Chesapeake Bay sealed the fate of the British army trapped in Yorktown in 1781. De Grasse lost the Battle of the Saints and was captured by Admiral Rodney in April 1782, an event which prevented a Franco-Spanish assault on Jamaica and not much else. The British press of the time (and historians since) made much of this battle; but while it did check the French, it certainly did not vanquish them, or their Spanish allies. And in the Indian Ocean, Admiral Suffren, a brilliant naval tactician, kept the Royal Navy on the defensive.

Reforms in the Colonial army

Colonial troops were a separate entity from the metropolitan army and the marines. The various army orders on uniforms, weapons, composition of units, pay, awards, etc., did not apply to colonial troops, who had their own regulations on such matters. For instance, a colonial officer did not need to have blue blood (but being the son of a colonial officer was a considerable advantage), so that the hated 1781 *noblesse* regulation in the metropolitan army did not apply. And, as we will see below, they had distinctive uniforms.

During the *Ancien Régime* the minister of the navy was also responsible for the colonies which were administered by the crown. We have seen above that colonial troops almost ceased to exist by the end of the Seven Years' War, most being incorporated into the army. From the end of 1762 Choiseul designated a number of army regiments to serve as garrisons in the colonies. Apart from being rather unpopular with the army, this led to administrative difficulties, with paper battles between the bureaucracies of the army and the colonial side of the ministry of the navy. Colonists did not like it either; they had been used to seeing troops belonging to their colony, with officers often coming from the colonial gentry rather than the somewhat disdainful nobility of France. By 1766 it was resolved to raise a 'Legion' per colony, but only those of Îsle-de-France and Saint-Domingue came into being. The Leeward Islands of Martinique and Guadeloupe continued to have army troops, while Guyana and Senegal each had a colonial battalion. With the *Compagnie des Indes* (French East India Company) closing its books in 1770 the crown took over its responsibilities, which included keeping garrisons in southern India.

On 18 August 1772 the colonial army was considerably reorganised. The regiments of Du Cap and

Engineers officers served with the French forces in all theatres of operations during the war. The uniform of the Corps royal du génie *was a blue coat with black collar, cuffs and lapels piped with red, red turnbacks, waistcoat and breeches, gold buttons, epaulettes and hat lace as shown on this c. 1776 illustration. (Anne S. K. Brown Military Collection, Brown University, Providence, USA)*

Port-au-Prince were created to serve in Saint-Domingue, those of Martinique and Guadeloupe to serve in the Leeward Islands, and those of Île-de-France, Port-Louis and Île-de-Bourbon to serve in the French islands of the Indian Ocean. On 30 December the regiment of Pondichery was raised to serve in India. The new regiments were to be of two battalions, incorporating whatever troops were in the colony and boosted by some recruits. While this worked in the West Indies, the East Indian regiments were very weak. On 21 January 1775 the regiments of Port-Louis and Île-de-Bourbon were abolished and incorporated into the Île-de-France regiment, which was boosted to 4 battalions. The Pondichery regiment's 2nd Battalion was never raised, but it was compensated for by a battalion of Sepoys. Also raised on 30 December 1772 was the three-company *Volontaires de Benyowski* to serve in Madagascar, and a company of invalids to be stationed in Île-de-France. Benyowski's volunteers, named after a Polish adventurer who had convinced the court (and himself) that a vast new colony could be established in Madagascar, withered away, becoming an independent company in 1778, and its sickly survivors were evacuated and incorporated in the Île-de-France regiment in 1782. The battalion of *Troupes nationales de Cayenne* in French Guyana had 8 companies from 1775 raised to 10 in 1779. In Gorée, Senegal, was a 'half company' (50 men) of the *Volontaires d'Afrique*; while the islands of Saint-Pierre-et-Miquelon in the North Atlantic, south of Newfoundland, also had 50 men for a complete 'company'. There were also colonial artillery companies, called *Canonniers-Bombardiers*, in most colonies.

In spite of a lack of complete uniformity in organisation (this was achieved after the war), there were 15 battalions plus a number of companies of white troops with a battalion of Sepoys on duty in the colonies at the outbreak of the war. From 1775 the West Indian regiments and the Île-de-France regiment had a standard organisation. Each battalion had a company of grenadiers, a company of chasseurs and eight companies of fusiliers:

Grenadier or chasseur company: 1 captain, 1 first-lieutenant, 1 second-lieutenant, 1 *fourrier*, 2 sergeants, 4 corporals, 4 *appointés* (lance-corporals), 40 grenadiers or chasseurs, 1 drummer. Total: 55.
Fusilier company: 1 captain, 1 first-lieutenant, 1

This Ingénieurs-géographes *(topographical engineers) were a separate entity and had a distinctive uniform consisting of a dark blue coat with aurore (orange-red) collar, cuffs and lapels, white turnbacks, waistcoat and breeches, silver buttons and lace as illustrated on this* c. 1776 *illustration. (Anne S. K. Brown Military Collection, Brown University, Providence, USA)*

second-lieutenant, 1 *fourrier*, 4 sergeants, 8 corporals, 8 *appointés*, 56 fusiliers, 2 drummers. Total: 82.
Regimental staff: 1 colonel, 1 lieutenant-colonel, 1 drum-major. Each battalion had a staff of: 1 *chef de bataillon*, 1 major, 1 assistant major, 1 sub-assistant major, 2 ensigns.

The establishment of the Pondichery regiment in India was the same for the grenadier and chasseur companies but the eight fusilier companies had 80 fusiliers each. The eight fusilier companies of the *Troupes nationales de Cayenne* battalion in French Guyana had the same composition as the West Indian regiments and there was a small battalion staff of 1 major, 1 assistant major and 1 sub-assistant major. There were also 10 companies of colonial artillery, each of 105 officers and men, in the East and West Indies, plus a smaller company of 53 in Guyana. The colonial army thus had an establishment of over 12,000, although the actual strength was probably about 8,000–9,000 white officers and men in 1778.

As can be seen by the table below, a number of other units were raised during the war. The most famous is probably the Duke of Lauzun's Legion which served in the United States (notably in the cavalry fight near Yorktown where Lauzun's Legion hussars routed Tarleton's British Legion light dragoons). The unit was formed from the 2nd Legion of the *Volontaires étrangers de la Marine*. Like other corps, such as the *Volontaires de Nassau* or the *Volontaires du Luxembourg*, nearly all units raised in France for colonial service during the war were largely composed of foreigners, usually Germans.

There was a considerable novelty in the new colonial corps: most were composed of free non-white personnel. In the West Indies especially this represented a considerable evolution in policy, and it is not without interest to note that some of these units existed there until 1786. In the East Indies, Sepoy battalions were rapidly raised from 1782 when the French landed forces in southern India. The way they were raised is worthy of some consideration, as a battalion (or two) of Sepoys would be affiliated to a French battalion and assume its name (i.e. *Bataillon des Sipayes du régiment de l'Îsle-de-France*) and the regimental facings on the uniform coat.

Each colony also had a militia organisation in which all able-bodied white and free coloured men had to serve. They were divided into infantry, artillery and cavalry companies, subject to frequent duties—some of a civil nature, such as police or

Table 1: Colonial Troops 1778–1783

Unit	Place	Bn or Cos (1778)	Raised
Compagnie franche	St. Pierre & Miqu.	1 Co	1763
Vol. d'Afrique	Senegal	1/2 Cos	1763 (6 Cos from 1779)
Tr. Nat. Cayenne	Fr. Guyana	1 Bn	1764
Canonniers-bombardiers	Fr. Guyana	1 Co	1764
Canonniers-bombardiers	Île-de-France	3 Cos	1765
Canonniers-bombardiers	St. Domingue	3 Cos	1768
Invalides I-de-Fr.	Île-de-France	1 Co	1772
Regt Du Cap	St. Domingue	2 Bns	1772
Regt Port-au-Prince	St. Domingue	2 Bns	1772
Regt Martinique	Martinique	2 Bns	1772
Regt Guadeloupe	Guadeloupe	2 Bns	1772
Regt Îsle-de-France	Île-de-France	4 Bns	1772
Regt Pondichery	India	1 Bn	1772
Sepoys*	India	1 Bn	1773 (to 1778)
Canonniers-bombardiers	Martin. & Guad.	3 Cos	1774
Canonniers-bombardiers	India	1 Co	1776
Comp franche Madagasc.	Madagascar	1 Co	1778 (to 1781)
Volontaires de Bouillé	Martinique	1 Co	1778
Cadets de Saint-Pierre	Martinique	1 Co	1778
Cadets du Gros-Morne	Martinique	1 Co	1778
Vol. étranger de la Marine	America & India	3 Legions	1778
Volontaires de Nassau	France	1 Legion	1778 (to 1779)
Chasseurs-volontaires**	St. Domingue	2 Bns	1779
Grenadiers-volontaires	St. Domingue	4 Cos	1779 (to 1780)
Corps des Travailleurs****	Guadeloupe	3 Cos	1779
Comp. dét. artillerie	Île-de-France	1 Co	1779 (to 1781)
Volontaires de Bourbon***	Île-de-Bourbon	2 Cos	1779
Vol. étrangers de Lauzun	United States	1 Legion	1780
Chasseurs-royaux**	St Domingue	1 Bn	1780 (only)
Vol. de Luxembourg	Cape of Good Hope	8 Cos	1780 (to 1782)
Volontaires libres**	Guad. & Martin.	2 Bns	1782
Volontaires libres**	Marie-Galante	1 Co	1782
Canonniers-bombardiers	Demerary	1 Co	1782
Compagnie franche	Demerary	1 Co	1782
Sepoys*	India	3–4 Bns	1782
Sepoys* (Trincomalee)	Ceylon	1 Bn	1782
Volontaires indiens*	India	1 Co	1783 (only)
Sepoys*	India	3 Bns	1783

(* composed of Indians including part of the officers; ** composed of free blacks and mulatoes with white officers; *** a company of free blacks was added in Dec. 1782; **** black slaves with free black and mulato NCOs)

taking a census—and had to provide themselves with weapons and uniforms as much as possible. The colonial militias also saw many reforms and improvements during the 1760s and 1770s, and were in good shape when war broke out.

WAR WITH BRITAIN

From the outset, the increasing disputes between Britain and her North American colonies roused interest and sympathy in France. From 1775, when it became an armed conflict, it was felt prudent to send five metropolitan army battalions to reinforce the colonial troops in the West Indies. The United States of America proclaimed their independence on 4 July 1776, but there was no way to tell which way the struggle would go. French intellectuals delighted at the wording of the American Declaration of Independence; businessmen were starting to wonder about a possible new market; and the general public started to hope for revenge against 'perfidious Albion'. At court, ministers and officials were cautious, and wished to see the resolve of the Americans tested before embarking on a war with Britain. However, foreign minister Count de Vergennes was arranging secretly via the playwright Beaumarchais for artillery, small arms, uniforms and other supplies to be sent to the Americans. Vergennes was also using every device he could to isolate Britain from her traditional allies. Then came the news of the British disaster at Saratoga in October 1777. Thereafter it was only a matter of time before the persuasive American ambassador to the French court, Benjamin Franklin, convinced France to recognise the United States, which was done by a treaty of friendship and commerce on 6 February 1778.

The news was received coldly in London, which recalled its ambassador from France. War had not been declared yet, but Admiral d'Estaing's squadron was sent to reinforce the West Indies in April. On 17 June, off Brittany, several British ships attacked the French frigate *Belle-Poule*, but she fought them off and got away to a triumphant return in Brest. On 10 July, Louis XVI ordered his warships to 'give chase'

to those of the Royal Navy. The real war was on. It was a gamble for France, which had 52 ships of the line against Britain's 66. Fellow Bourbons in Spain hesitated for nearly a year before coming into the conflict on 8 May 1779, after which date the 58 Spanish ships of the line joined France's 63 against Britain's 90. In November 1780 Britain, which could find no allies, also declared war on Holland. In 1781 the lesser naval powers such as Denmark, Portugal, Sweden and Russia formed themselves into an 'Armed Neutrality', while Austria and Prussia would have nothing to do with the conflict. Count de Vergenne's diplomatic skills left Britain completely isolated. The war would be fought at sea and overseas.

Gunner of Royal-Artillerie, *1776 regulation uniform. The white epaulettes and square brass buckles shown on several figures of this manuscript remain puzzling details. Note the white waistcoat instead of the usual blue for the artillery. (Anne S. K. Brown Military Collection, Brown University, Providence, USA)*

The West Indies

In Martinique, the news of war arrived on 17 August, and the energetic 38-year-old Governor-General Marquis de Bouillé set the tone. He gathered a mixed force of regulars and colonial volunteers and militias on a few frigates, and captured Dominica—the British island between Martinique and Guadeloupe—on 7 September. Reinforcements poured in from France and Britain, but the French kept the initiative in the smaller islands while the Spanish concentrated on Louisiana and West Florida. By 1782 the only British islands left were Barbados, Antigua, St. Lucia and Jamaica. Some 27 French metropolitan infantry battalions, beside smaller detachments and artillery, had joined the 8 colonial infantry battalions plus the colonial artillery and volunteers in the West Indies.

The United States

The first actions by French troops on American soil were at the siege of Savannah during September and October of 1779, which ended in failure. But 5,000 officers and men—the equivalent of about 9 battalions of infantry and artillery with 300 of Lauzun's Legion hussars—under the command of Count

Rochambeau arrived at Newport, Rhode Island, in July 1780. This force, placed under the supreme command of General George Washington, considerably impressed the Americans as it marched south in 1781, slowly isolating Lord Cornwallis in Yorktown by September. They were joined by 3,000 more troops which had come up from the West Indies in Admiral de Grasse's fleet, making the besieging Franco-American army some 16,000 strong. The 7,000 British and mercenary Hessian troops marched out to the tune of 'The World Turned Upside-Down' on 19 October. Thereafter military operations in the United States almost stopped. The British evacuated Savannah in July and Charleston in December 1782, while most of the French expeditionary corps (except

◀ *Private of a Miner company of* Royal-Artillerie, *1776–79, in undress wearing the blue trimmed with scarlet pokalem fatigue cap, white belted waistcoat with red cuffs and holding a pick. The dress uniform was the same as gunners but with aurore epaulettes. (Anne S. K. Brown Military Collection, Brown University, Providence, USA)*

▶ *Driver of* Royal-Artillerie, *1776 regulation uniform, wearing dark blue coat and breeches, scarlet turnbacks, sky-blue collar, cuffs and lapels, brass buttons. (Anne S. K. Brown Military Collection, Brown University, Providence, USA)*

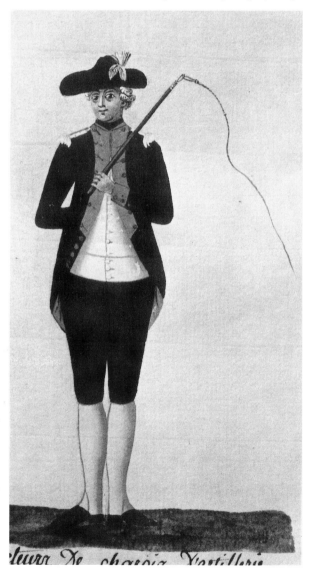

for Lauzun's Legion) left from Boston bound for the West Indies on 23 December. Only New York remained to the British.

The East Indies

From August to October 1778 the French posts in India were all captured and the Pondichery regiment was sent to France. The 4 battalions of colonial troops in Île-de-France were joined in July 1780 by the 2nd Battalion of the Austrasie regiment. The 1st Battalion with the 3rd Legion of the *Volontaires étrangers de la Marine* arrived in October 1781. On 25 February 1782, Austrasie, the 3rd Legion, 1,500 men of the Îsle-de-France regiment, the *Volontaires de Bourbon* and artillery landed at Porto-Novo in India and joined the forces of Hyder-Ali, which attached Sepoys to each French battalion. These troops were also used by Admiral Suffren as marines and for the capture of Trincomalee in Ceylon during August 1782.

The Marquis de Bussy, an aged veteran of India from the Seven Years' War, was in command of 4 more infantry battalions and an artillery brigade (2,300 men) sent from France. They landed in India on 19 March 1783, and Sepoys were likewise attached to them. Tipoo Sultan, son of Hyder-Ali, was also there with his army. The British force of 15,000 men, including 3,500 European troops, under General Stuart was losing control of the military situation in southern India and tried to contain the French in Cuddelore on 13 June; but much of the 102nd Foot was destroyed in the process. Admiral Hughes was beaten off by Suffren, which made Stuart's position critical; but luckily for him a British frigate arrived on 29 June with news that the preliminaries for peace had been signed in Europe on 20 January. Most historians contend that, without naval power, Stuart's demoralised force could have been beaten by the Franco-Indian forces and southern India lost to Britain.

Other areas

In late 1781, 8 battalions of infantry with artillery were sent to Minorca to help the Spanish capture the British stronghold of Fort St. Philip at Mahon. The brave British garrison of 3,000 held out for 30 days

Model of a French Gribeauval system 8 Pounder field gun with carriage and limber. Such guns were brought overseas by the army Royal-Artillerie corps. Note that the tube is in the rear set of trunnion holes, which was done when in a "travelling" position. Photo by Raoul Brunon. (Bibliothèque Raoul & Jean Brunon, Musée de l'Armée. Château de l'Empéri, Salon-de-Provence, France)

At left a Canonnier garde-côtes, *1778–83, wearing a dark blue coat with sea-green lapels, turnbacks, waistcoat, breeches and brass buttons. Some 23,000 men of this militia coast artillery corps were embodied for part-time service in France's coastal batteries during the war. At right, a Royal-Artillerie waggon driver according to the 1779 dress regulations wearing a dark blue coat with sky-blue collar and cuffs, no lapels, red turnbacks and piping, dark blue waistcoat and breeches and brass buttons. From a reconstruction by Philippoteaux. (National Archives of Canada, C33798)*

but capitulated on 5 February 1782. The Duke de Crillon, a French officer in the service of Spain, was responsible for this success and was put in command of the army besieging Gibraltar. The French regiments were transferred from Minorca to Algeciras in June, joining some 39 Spanish battalions in a combined force of about 28,000. General Elliot's 7,000 British troops were well entrenched in one of the world's finest fortresses. French engineer Colonel d'Arçon devised some 'unsinkable and unburnable' floating batteries to breach the seaward side. A general attack was made on 13 September but, unsupported by the Admiral Cordoba's ships, some floating batteries were set on fire by British red hot

shot, and the attempt ended in failure. Thereafter, the siege became more like a blockade.

As can be seen in the chronology above, French forces were also active in Senegal, Dutch Guyana, Pensacola and Hudson's Bay. In July 1781, the Pondichery regiment and the *Canonniers-bombardiers de l'Inde*[2] arrived with Admiral Suffren at Cape Town and remained there to reinforce the Dutch garrison. They were joined by the *Volontaires du Luxembourg* in May 1782 — a French colonial corps transferred to Dutch colonial service the previous month. The troops in South Africa saw no action.

UNIFORMS

The metropolitan army

Choiseul's reforms had a considerable influence on the appearance of the army after the Seven Years' War. Gone were the somewhat carefree ways; uniforms were regulated with precision down to the last button, which was stamped with the regiment's number from December 1762. Increasingly complex regulations appeared in 1767, when white cockades were at last made universal, and again on 2 September 1775. The French line infantry was dressed in white coats. The foreign regiments wore red coats in the Irish and Swiss units, and 'dark sky blue' coats in the German units.

The most controversial uniform order was devised by Count Saint-Germain and became regulation on 31 May 1776. It was a radical departure from the usual cut, and featured a closed coat with short tails and even a 'four-cornered' hat. Count Saint-Germain was well intentioned, but his 'Prussian' uniform was met with a hail of protests and jeers.

It consisted of a short-tailed coat with lapels, each having seven small buttons, and four buttons below which could be fastened; two buttons on the cuff and two above it; shoulder straps buttoned at the top of the shoulder; a small standing collar; and horizontal pockets. The facing colour was applied to the lapels, cuffs, turnbacks and the piping of the shoulder straps and pockets. The coat collar was usually of a different colour. The white waistcoat was a very light affair

---

[2] A 25-man detachment of this unit went with Bussy's force to India in 1783.

18

with no sleeves, no lining and with cloth buttons. A white cloth belt was introduced about 20cm wide which had two rows of four cloth buttons to fasten it. The breeches were white with cloth buttons. The white gaiters had no garter and buttoned to the breeches at the knee; and in the winter a pair of black gaiters ending below the knees was also to be worn. The 'four-cornered' hat was considered by critics to be of Prussian inspiration and especially ugly, although its unusual shape was meant, according to the regulation, to give protection against rain. It was of black felt laced with black, and featured a small plume: white for fusiliers, red and white for grenadiers, green and white for chasseurs (see Plate A).

Another garment introduced in 1776 was the *redingote*, which was a frock with two rows of six large uniform buttons in front, with the cuffs and the collar of the respective facing colours as on the coat—a good idea, but not retained in 1779. The fatigue cap was an ingenious affair called a *pokalem*, with a front turn-up and a turban which could be brought down over the ears and tied under the chin in bad weather. It was of

Table 2: Metropolitan army infantry battalions serving overseas 1778–1783

Regiment	Location	Number of Bns.	Sent	Returned
Auxerrois	Martinique	1	Nov 1775	July 1783
Viennois	Martinique	1	Nov 1775	July 1783
Armagnac	Guadeloupe	1	Nov 1775	July 1783
Agenois	St. Domingue	1	Nov 1775	July 1783
Cambrésis	St. Domingue	1	Nov 1775	July 1783
Gâtinois	Martinique	1	Nov 1775	July 1783
Gâtinois	St. Domingue	1	Oct 1777	July 1783
Agenois	St. Domingue	1	Oct 1777	July 1783
Viennois	Martinique	1	Oct 1777	July 1783
Auxerrois	Guadeloupe	1	Oct 1777	July 1783
Armagnac	Guadeloupe	1	Oct 1777	July 1783
Walsh	Martinique	1	April 1778	March 1784
Hainault	Martinique	1	April 1778	1783
Champagne	Martinique	1	Jan 1779	July 1783
Dillon	Martinique	1	March 1779	Sept 1783
Foix	Martinique	1	July 1779	1783
Austrasie	India	1	Jan 1780	April 1785
Enghien	Martinique	2	Feb 1780	July 1783
Tourraine	Martinique	2	Feb 1780	July 1783
Royal-Comtois	Martinique	1	Feb 1780	Feb 1784
Soissonois	United States	2	May 1780	July 1783
Bourbonnois	United States	2	May 1780	June 1783
Saintonge	United States	2	May 1780	June 1783
Royal-Deux-Ponts	United States	2	May 1780	June 1783
Austrasie	India	1	March 1781	April 1785
Lyonnois	Mahon & Gibraltar	2	Oct 1781	April 1783
Bretagne	Mahon & Gibraltar	2	Oct 1781	April 1783
Bouillon	Mahon & Gibraltar	2	Oct 1781	April 1783
Royal-Suèdois	Mahon & Gibraltar	2	Oct 1781	April 1783
La Mark	India	2	Dec 1781	April 1785
Aquitaine	India	1	Dec 1781	July 1785
Royal-Roussillon	India	1	Dec 1781	July 1785
Rl-Hesse-Darmstadt	West Indies	1	Dec 1781	April 1783
Auvergne	Martinique	2	Sept 1782	July 1783
Berwick	Martinique	1	Sept 1782	1783
Rouergue	West Indies	2	Nov 1782	April 1783

(In October 1777 a company of Dragoons from each regiment of Condé and Belsunce were sent to Saint-Domingue and returned in 1783; from March 1781 to September 1782, nearly 11,000 men—the equivalent of about 17 battalions—from various regiments were sent to the West Indies.)

Fusilier of the La Reine Regiment, 1776 regulation uniform. The epaulettes are shown with fringes but the regulation stated a button instead. (Anne S. K. Brown Military Collection, Brown University, Providence, USA)

Officer's gilded brass plate for a fur grenadier cap. Officially abolished during 1775 in the army, the popular fur caps were not given up by many units. For instance, the grenadiers of Soissonnois were seen parading with these caps in Philadelphia in September 1781. Photo by Raoul Brunon. (Bibliothèque Raoul & Jean Brunon, Musée de l'Armée. Château de l'Empéri, Salon-de-Provence, France)

the coat colour, with piping and a lily on the front turn-up of the coat lapel colour (see Plate H). The *pokalem* must have been popular, for it featured again in the 1779 and 1786 regulations.

The Prince de Montbarrey became minister in September 1777, and quickly cancelled the most unusual features of the 1776 uniform while preparing a new regulation which finally appeared in **February 1779**. As a result, it is next to impossible to know exactly to what extent individual regiments took into wear the 1776 uniform. Coats were to last up to three

years but hats, waistcoats, breeches and most other items were a yearly issue. We also note that coats were delivered to regiments not in one shipment for everyone at once, but a third being replaced every year. It was therefore theoretically possible in late 1776 for a regiment to be seen wearing three different uniforms at the same time. By 1780 the odds were down to two, and we have found evidence of this in at least one case: the Saintonge regiment during 1780–1781. Further research would probably reveal other examples.

Just how far was the unpopular 1776 uniform actually adopted? Evidence is scanty, but the order book of the Boulonnois regiments suggests no great rush. In August, the regiment paraded still wearing the pre-1775 leather helmet, and right up to the end of the order book in late October 1776 the enlisted men appear to have been unaffected. Only recruits entering the regiment were given old militia uniforms altered by regimental tailors to the new regulation with crimson lapels, cuffs and turnbacks, pink collar and white metal buttons stamped '82'. The regiment's officers were ordered on 4 September to have the new model hats and to have new coats made or the old ones altered according to the regulation. In practice, it appears that officers in most regiments continued to wear the old coats with the new facing colours on lapels, cuffs and collars. This at least is what is inferred by Captain d'Aleyrac of the Languedoc regiment, when he mentioned that 'among other variations, we took [into wear] aurore collar, cuffs and lapels, white metal buttons with No. 70', but did not say anything about aurore turnbacks or strange hats.

A crude drawing of the Royal Deux-Ponts regiment by Captain Von Closen shows a back view of a

Table 3: Metropolitan Royal-Artillerie serving overseas 1778–1783

Regiment	Location	Number	Sent	Returned
Metz	West Indies	1 Bn	Oct 1777	1783
Metz	United States	2 Cos	May 1780	June 1783
Auxonne	United States	1 Bn	May 1780	June 1783
Metz	India	1 Co	March 1781	April 1785(?)
Metz	United States	4 Cos	1781	1783
Grenoble	Martinique	1 Co	1781	1783
Besançon	Mahon & Gibraltar	2 Cos	Oct 1781	April 1783
Strasbourg	Mahon & Gibraltar	1/2 Cos	Oct 1781	April 1783
Besançon	India	4 Cos	Oct 1781	March 1786
La Fère	West Indies	4 Cos	1782	1783

private in the 1776 uniform, with a note concerning the 'four-cornered hat', and a figure dated 1778 which shows an enlisted man wearing the more conventional hat, waistcoat and coat with white turnbacks. Obviously, Montbarrey's arrival at the ministry brought a sigh of relief to this regiment and many others. A witness to the attack on Grenada in July 1779 shows figures of metropolitan infantry in white coats with long tails and white turnbacks. But some units obviously had the original 1776 uniform even overseas, as the same painting shows men of the

Dillon (Irish) regiment charging up a hill wearing a short red coat with yellow turnbacks (see Plate B).

Another item that was abolished in 1776 was the fur cap of the grenadiers, but this order was ignored in some regiments, for we find that the Soissonnois grenadiers parading in Philadelphia in 1781 with 'its grenadiers' caps with great rose and white plumes, impressed the fair sex greatly' according to Von Closen (see Plate E). It seems that Hainault's grenadiers kept their bearskins also. Such evidence is surely only the tip of the iceberg, as the officials eventually gave up and allowed the caps to grenadiers again in 1788. In the list of facings below, because of limited space, we have given only those regiments listed in our Chronology of actions up to the end of 1781.

Table 4: 31 May 1776 Dress Regulation facings for the infantry:

Regiment	Lapels & cuffs	Collar	Buttons
3 Champagne	silver-grey	silver-grey	yellow
4 Austrasie	silver-grey	red	white
6 Armagnac	sky-blue	aurore	white
9 Normandie	black	yellow	yellow
10 Neustrie	black	pink	white
12 Auxerrois	black	crimson	yellow
14 Agénois	pink	green	white
15 Bourbonnois	crimson	crimson	yellow
16 Forès	crimson	green	white
17 Auvergne	violet	violet	yellow
18 Gatinois	violet	yellow	yellow
20 Cambrésis	violet	pink	white
22 Viennois	red*	green	yellow
25 Brie	steel-grey	steel-grey	white
26 Poitou	sky-blue	pink	yellow
30 Dauphin	blue	pink	yellow
34 Touraine	steel-grey	yellow	white
36 Aquitaine	sky-blue	yellow	yellow
41 Soissonnois	red*	sky-blue	yellow
42 La Reine	red	blue	white
51 Hainault	crimson	yellow	yellow
52 La Sarre	yellow	red	white
56 Condé	red	yellow	yellow
70 Languedoc	aurore	aurore	white
71 Beauce	aurore	green	yellow
76 Royal-Comtois	sky-blue	crimson	yellow
85 Saintonge	aurore	sky-blue	white
86 Foix	dark green	yellow	yellow
96 Enghein	aurore	red	white

(* indicates red 'speckled with white' facing colour)

Foreign regiments:

Regiment	Coat	Lapels & cuffs	Collar	Buttons
90 Dillon (Irish)	red	yellow	white	yellow*
95 Walsh (Irish)	red	blue	yellow	yellow*
104 Royal Deux-Ponts (G.)	sky-blue	crimson	crimson	white

(* indicates that the cuff buttons were set herringbone fashion. The buttonholes are variously shown in twist cord of the ground colour or laced with white.)

The 1779 uniform

The royal order of 21 February 1779, nearly eight months after the beginning of hostilities, at last prescribed the official replacement for Saint-Germain's unpopular garments. The spirit of the whole new order of dress was one of moderation and a return to the *à la française* cut and style. A wise move: the men of the proud French army felt that they looked like Prussians rather than Frenchmen in the 1776 uniform, and this 1779 order gave them back what they felt should be their national fashion (see Plates E & G).

The white coat was more ample, with long tails and white turnbacks ornamented with lilies, grenades or bugle horns in the facing colour for fusilier, grenadier or chasseur companies respectively. Facing colour could be applied to the lapels and cuffs, or to cuffs only, or to lapels only. The lapels or cuffs which were not faced were of white edged with piping in the facing colour. The three-pointed pocket flaps of regiments with yellow metal buttons were horizontal, but those of regiments with white metal buttons were vertical; all were piped in the facing colour. The collar for all (except foreign regiments) was white, and while the order is silent as to piping illustrations of the period nearly always show piping of the facing colour. Each lapel had seven small buttons and there were three large ones below the right lapel. The cuffs were as previously, with two small buttons on the cuff and two above; but the opening above the cuff was now piped in the facing colour. The shoulder straps were white piped with the facing colour for fusiliers, green piped white for chasseurs, and red piped white for grenadiers. In many regiments the grenadiers continued to wear red fringed epaulettes.

The hat was a more usual tricorn, which was well on the way to becoming a bicorn, with the front raised high. It was laced with black; the cockade was white with a black loop fastened to a small regimental button. Plumes were abolished, but grenadiers (who did wear hats) had a red tuft as a distinction; fusiliers and chasseurs were to have plain hats. The waistcoat was white and of a conventional cut with sleeves, a small standing collar, pocket flaps and small regimental buttons. The collar and cuffs of the waistcoat were of the facing colour if the regiment had coat lapels and cuffs of the facing colour, waistcoat collar only if the facing was on coat lapels only, and waistcoat cuffs only if the facing was on the coat cuffs only. The cloth belt was abolished. The breeches were white, and the long gaiters were of the conventional sort with garters—each man had one pair made of white linen, one pair of blackened linen, and one

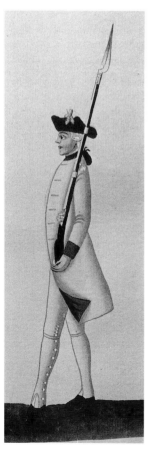

Fusilier of the Saintonge Regiment, 1776 regulation uniform, wearing the short-lived redingote but this manuscript shows the lining to be of the facing colour which is possible but unlikely to have been general practice. (Anne S. K. Brown Military Collection, Brown University, Providence, USA)

pair black woollen cloth. The *pokalem* was as before but piping was only applied to the edge of the front turn-up.

We have seen above that clothing was issued to a third of each unit every year so that, in theory, all the men in a regiment would have the new uniform by the end of 1781. The supplies for the troops going to the United States in 1780 included their 'complete clothing', so that only in 1782 would the expeditionary corps need a complete supply of breeches, gaiters, shirts, stockings and shoes only. This could be taken to indicate that everybody had the new uniform; but in fact, it was probably only by spring or summer 1781 that all the enlisted men of Bourbonnois, Soissonnois, Royal Deux-Ponts and Royal-Artillerie wore the 1779 uniform. During the Yorktown campaign the regimental stores indicate facing cloth of the new regulation only for these regiments. But Saintonge had some of its men in the 1776 facing colours: according to regimental records, only 226 'bad' coats were issued in 1779, 290 in 1780 and 550 in 1781. Regimental stores carried aurore cloth suitable for repairs to lapels and cuffs, as well as 'natural' green cloth for the new facing colour. Possibly a couple of hundred men of Saintonge might have had the aurore facings at Yorktown, which would explain why the American gunner Madeira recalled Saintonge in 'red' facings many years later and the other regiments in their proper 1779 facings. James Thacher, another American soldier, saw Saintonge in 'white broadcloth, trimmed with green' in July and September 1781. As the regimental clothing record shows, both men were right (see Plate E).

The hue of the facing colour is sometimes given by observers. Von Closen described Soissonnois' crimson as 'rose-coloured lapels and facings' when it paraded in Philadelphia on 4 September 1781. This was obviously not the very dark British crimson but rather of the lighter pink shade, probably very much like the crimson facings of Napoleon's Polish lancers of the Imperial Guard. What may have been the violet lapels of Gatinois were seen as 'white coats turned up with blue' near Yorktown in early September 1781. Viennois' steel-grey cuffs were seen in 1782 as 'white cuffed with blue', and it was indeed a blue-grey hue. In the list of facings (Table 5), because of limited space, we have given only those regiments listed in our Chronology of actions from 1779.

Table 5: 21 February 1779 Dress Regulations facings for the infantry:

Regiment	Lapels	Cuffs	Buttons
6 Armagnac	sky-blue	white	white
7 Champagne	white	sky-blue	white
8 Austrasie	black	black	yellow
12 Auxerrois	black	white	white
13 Bourbonnois	white	black	white
14 Forèz	violet	violet	yellow
16 Agenois	white	violet	yellow
17 Auvergne	violet	violet	white
18 Gatinois	violet	white	white
20 Cambrésis	steel-grey	steel-grey	yellow
22 Viennois	white	steel-grey	yellow
25 Brie	steel-grey	steel-grey	white
26 Poitou	steel-grey	white	white
28 Lyonnois	pink	pink	yellow
34 Touraine	white	pink	white
36 Aquitaine	yellow	white	yellow
41 Soissonnois	crimson	crimson	yellow
47 Bretagne	white	crimson	yellow
51 Hainault	white	crimson	white
52 La Sarre	silver-grey	silver-grey	yellow
55 Royal-Roussillon	royal-blue	royal-blue	white
59 Rouergue	silver-grey	silver-grey	white
71 Beauce	aurore	white	yellow
76 Royal-Comtois	white	royal-blue	white
78 Monsieur	scarlet	scarlet	white*
85 Saintonge	white	green	yellow
86 Foix	green	green	white
96 Enghien	white	white	white*

(* indicates scarlet turnbacks)

Foreign regiments:

Regiment	Coat	Lapels & cuffs	Collar	Buttons
80 La Mark (German)	sky-blue	yellow	red	white
90 Dillon (Irish)	red	yellow	white	yellow*
92 Royal-Suedois (Ger.)	sky-blue	buff	buff	yellow
91 Berwick (Irish)	red	black	yellow	white*
95 Walsh (Irish)	red	blue	yellow	yellow*
97 Rl-Hesse-Darmstadt (G)	sky-blue	capucine	capucine	white[3]
103 Bouillon (Ger.)	sky-blue	white	white	yellow
104 Royal Deux-Ponts (G.)	sky-blue	yellow	sky-blue	white

(* indicates that the cuff buttons were set herringbone fashion. The buttonholes are variously shown in twist cord of the ground colour or laced with white.)

[3] Previous to 15 April 1780, this regiment was Royal-Bavière and had black facings.

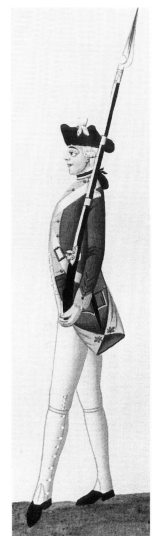

Fusilier private of the Dillon (Irish) regiment 1776 regulation uniform. The short red coat with yellow collar, cuffs, lapels, pocket piping and turnbacks (with a red lily) is showed along with the peculiar "herringbone" setting of the brass buttons on the cuffs and lower sleeve, the buttonholes there being trimmed with red twist cord. According to the regulation, fusiliers had shoulder straps rather than the white fringed epaulettes. In practice, the bayonet belt appears to have been often worn around the waist. (Anne S. K. Brown Military Collection, Brown

Royal-Artillerie

The 1776 uniform was blue coat with blue collar and lapels, red cuffs, piping and turnbacks, blue shoulder straps piped red, and yellow metal buttons; white short waistcoat and cloth belt; blue breeches; hat laced black with white plume; blue *redingote* with red cuffs and blue collar piped red. The Miners had an aurore shoulder strap and the *Ouvriers* companies had red lapels. The 1779 uniform had the same colours except for the waistcoat, which was now blue, and the hat plume was abolished (see Plates C & D).

Marines and Bombardiers

On 26 December 1774 the *Corps royal d'infanterie de la Marine* were assigned a blue coat with red collar, boot cuffs and lapels, blue turnbacks, yellow metal buttons (three to each cuff and pocket, seven to each lapel and three below the right lapel); blue waistcoat and breeches; black hat laced yellow; white gaiters in summer, black in winter. On the same day the three companies of *Bombardiers de la Marine* were assigned a blue coat with red collar, cuffs, lapels, turnbacks, waistcoat and breeches, yellow metal buttons (three under each cuff and to each pocket, seven to each lapel and three below the right lapel), and bearskin caps with brass plates (see Plate H).

Colonial infantry and artillery

The colonial regular troops had their own regulations regarding uniforms and were not subject to anything contrived by the ministry of war; they thus escaped Saint-Germain's 'Prussian' uniform. Indeed, for most of them, there were few official changes between 1772 and 1786.

The regular colonial infantry regiments in the West Indies had a blue coat with no lapels but with turned-down collar, cuffs and shoulder strap of the facing colour; white turnbacks; white metal buttons set as follows: six large in front (one at the neck, two at the chest and three at the waist), three large to each pocket, one large to each back hip, four small buttons on each boot cuff, and one small to the shoulder strap of fusiliers. Fringed epaulettes were of the regimental facing colour for grenadiers and white for chasseurs. The facing colours were: Du Cap, Saxon green; Port-au-Prince, red; Martinique, buff; Guadeloupe, crimson. Illustrations of the period show the facings and the front edged with white piping and cloth anchors of the facing colour on the turnbacks, white waistcoat, breeches and gaiters; black tricorn laced white with white cockade, cockade loop and small white metal button (see Plate B).

From 12 March 1779, the battalion of *Troupes nationales de Cayenne* in French Guyana had the same uniform as above except for three small buttons under the cuffs, ten large buttons down the front, blue cuffs and red collar. The previous uniform was white with blue collar, cuffs and lapels, white metal buttons.

In the East Indies, the regular colonial infantry wore a white coat with turned-down collar, cuffs and lapels of the regimental facing colour—blue for Îsle-de-France (see Plate F) and orange for Pondichery; white turnbacks; white metal buttons: three large below the right lapel, three large to each pocket, three small under each cuff, six small to each lapel, and one small to the shoulder strap of fusiliers. Fringed epaulettes were of the regimental facing colour for grenadiers and red for chasseurs. White waistcoat, breeches and gaiters; black tricorn laced white with white cockade, cockade loop and small white metal button. The facings of Pondichery were changed to white collar with blue cuffs and lapels in 1780, but these had worn out at the Cape of Good Hope by

Fusilier private of the Walsh (Irish) regiment, 1776 regulation uniform. The short red coat with yellow collar and blue cuffs, lapels, pocket piping and turnbacks (with a red lily) is showed along with the peculiar "herringbone" setting of the brass buttons on the cuffs and lower sleeve, the buttonholes there being trimmed with red twist cord. According to the regulation, fusiliers had shoulder straps rather than the white fringed epaulettes. In practice, the bayonet belt appears to have been often worn around the waist. (Anne S. K. Brown Military Collection, Brown University, Providence, USA)

1: Volontaire, Cadets de Saint-Pierre 1778
2: Chasseur, Regiment de Viennois, 1778
3: Officer, Martinique Militia,
   Fort-Royal Battalion, c. 1778-80

A

1: Grenadier, Martinique Regiment, 1778-83
2: Fusilier, Dillon's (Irish) Regiment, 1779
3: Volunteer Chasseurs-volontaires
   de Saint-Domingue, 1779

B

1: Hussar, Volontaires étrangers
de la Marine, 1778–83
2: Gunner, Royal-Artillerie, 1779–83
3: Infantry private, 1st Legion, Volontaire
étrangers de la Marine, 1778–82

C

1: Hussar, Lauzun's Legion, USA, 1780-83
2: Gunner, Royal-Artillerie, c. 1780-83
3: Infantry corporal, Lauzun's Legion,
   USA, 1780-82

D

1: Grenadier, Bourbonnois Regiment,
   USA 1780-82
2: Drummer, Royal Deux-Ponts (German)
   Regiment, USA, 1780-82
3: Fusilier, Saintonge Regiment,
   USA, 1780-81
4: Chasseur, Saintonge Regiment,
   USA, 1780-82

1: Sepoy, Isle-de-France Regiment, India, 1782-83
2: Fusilier, Isle-de-France Regiment, India, 1782-83
3: Sepoy, Austrasie, Regiment, India, 1782-83

F

1: Fusilier, Volontaires de Bourbon, 1779-83
2: Drummer, La Mark (German) Regiment,
   India, 1783
3: Officer, Aquitaine Regiment, India, 1783

1: Officer, French Navy, 1778–83
2: Bombardier, Bombardiers de la Marine, 1778–83
3: Fusilier, Corps royal de l'infanterie de la Marine, 1778–83
4: Fusilier, Barrois Regiment, 1776–82

H

March 1783 when plain blue coats with linen lining were procured locally.

The six colonial artillery companies in the West Indies (*Canonniers-bombardiers*) had a blue single-breasted coat with red turned-down collar, boot cuffs and turnbacks; yellow metal buttons: four large to each cuff, 12 large down the front, three to each pocket, and a small one to the aurore epaulette. The hat was laced yellow and the small waistcoat buttons were of yellow metal, but other items were the same as the infantry. In French Guyana, the *Canonniers-bombardiers de la Guyane* had blue turnbacks and waistcoats, white breeches, and the coat had red lapels with six small buttons each and three small buttons under each cuff. For the *Canonniers-bombardiers de l'Île-de-France* the turnbacks, waistcoat and breeches were blue, the lapels red with six small buttons each and three small buttons under each cuff. In India, the *Canonniers-bombardiers de l'Inde* had a blue single-breasted coat with red turned-down collar and boot cuffs; blue turnbacks; yellow metal buttons: three large to each cuff, 12 large down the front, three to each pocket, and a small one to the yellow epaulette (after October 1780, red lapels with six small buttons were allowed). Blue waistcoat and breeches. At the Cape of Good Hope since 1781 their worn-out uniforms were replaced by white nankeen waistcoat and breeches in March 1783, blue coats with red cuffs and piping and crude linen smocks and trousers in August.

Foreign volunteers raised in Europe

Of the new colonial corps raised in France during the war, the *Volontaires étrangers de la Marine* had the most elaborate uniforms, prescribed on 1 September 1778 (see Plate C). The infantry had a sky-blue coat with lemon yellow cuffs and lapels. The standing collar and epaulettes of the 1st Legion were lemon yellow, the 2nd Legion had white, the 3rd Legion had red. Turnbacks were grey; there were seven small white metal buttons to each lapel, two below the cuff and two below the sleeve, four large below the right lapel. White waistcoat with 12 small buttons and three to each pocket; white breeches and gaiters; hat laced white for fusiliers, and bearskin cap without a plate for grenadiers, black cockades and black cravats. The hussars attached to each Legion had sky-blue dolmans with lemon yellow cuffs and breeches all trimmed with white braid, sky-blue pelisse with lemon yellow cuffs and a lemon yellow cloth border (instead of fur) trimmed with white braid, all buttons being white metal. The cap was a black felt 'schako' (a mirleton) trimmed with yellow lace. The '*Compagnie générale*' was the HQ hussar company and also had sky-blue dolman and pelisse with lemon yellow cuffs, but trimmed with yellow lace and yellow metal buttons. The breeches were scarlet, as was the edging of the pelisse.

On 5 March 1780 the 2nd Legion, which had

Grenadiers of the Royal Deux-Pont regiment after a naïve drawing by Baron Ludgwig Von Closen, an officer in the unit. The figure to the left shows a back view wearing the 1776 uniform worn under the Saint-Germain ministry, the notation referring to the "four cornered hat" and the leather queue bag. The figure to the right is dated 1778 and reveals the changes to a more conventional uniform allowed by the Prince of Montbarrey from late 1777, which became official from February 1779. The original drawing appears to be lost but these black and white photos taken in the 1930s show a dark hue for the facings which would be the crimson of the 1776 regulations as the regiment took yellow, a much lighter hue in 1779. The piece of paper in the 1788 grenadier's hand appears to have been added later (rather clumsily) and has "Indép. d'Amé. 1783." written on. (Library of Congress)

33

stayed in France, was converted to become Lauzun's Legion (*Volontaires étrangers de Lauzun*) and soon left for the US with Rochambeau's army in May. The infantry kept the same uniform but the hussars adopted the uniform of the *Compagnie générale* (see Plate D).

The short-lived *Volontaires de Nassau* (10 December 1778–15 August 1779) had dark blue coat with orange collar, cuffs and lapels and white metal buttons. The *Volontaires du Luxembourg* (1 October 1780, transferred to Dutch service 30 April 1782) had blue coat with white collar, cuffs and lapels and yellow metal buttons.

West Indian volunteer corps

The *Volontaires de Bouillé* (1 July 1778–12 June 1784) had a blue short coat, red cuffs, plain brass buttons, 'a helmet, a short waistcoat, linen breeches', and black gaiters. The *Cadets de Saint-Pierre* (1 July 1778–c. 1783) had blue with yellow cuffs and silver lace (see Plate A). The *Cadets du Gros-Morne* (1 July

Fusilier of the Royal Deux-Pont regiment according to a 1778 print by Juillet dressed in a uniform of conventional "French" style. The coat is dark sky-blue with crimson collar, cuffs and lapels prescribed in 1776, but has long tails with white turnbacks. The hat is the usual tricorn with the white plumes of the 1776 regulation. (Anne S. K. Brown Military Collection, Brown University, Providence, USA)

1778–c. 1783) wore white with black cuffs, lapels and gaiters, white metal buttons, hat laced black with a black plume. The *Chasseurs-volontaires de Saint-Domingue* (12 March 1779–c. 1783) wore a blue coat with yellow standing collar, green cuffs, blue lapels, white turnbacks and white metal buttons, green epaulettes, white waistcoat and breeches, hat laced black with a white and yellow plume (see Plate B). The *Grenadiers-volontaires de Saint-Domingue* (12 March 1779–c. 1780) had a blue coat with red standing collar and cuffs, blue lapels, white turnbacks and white metal buttons, red epaulettes, white waistcoat and breeches, hat laced black with a white plume. The *Corps des Travailleurs de la Guadeloupe* (13 May 1779–c. 1783) wore blue faced with black, 'the same as sappers'. The *Chasseurs-royaux de Saint-Domingue* (26 May–5 October 1780) had a white linen short coat, boot cuffs, lapels, short waistcoat, gaiter-trousers, white metal buttons, yellow standing coat collar piped green, 'black Corsican hat of boiled leather with yellow and green plume', and red, yellow, green, blue or black epaulettes depending on company. The *Volontaires libres* (late 1782–1786) had a blue coat with yellow cuffs and lapels, grey linen turnbacks, white metal buttons, white waistcoat and gaiter-trousers, hat laced black with white cockade loop.

Indian Sepoys and volunteer corps

The battalion of Pondichery *Sipahis* or *Cipayes* (12 November 1773–October 1778) had a blue short coat, yellow collar, cuffs and lapels, white metal buttons, white waistcoat, white short trousers edged with blue, white turban. From late February 1782, when French troops landed in India, Sepoy battalions were raised and attached to each French battalion and dressed in uniforms of various colours with the facings of the French regiment. The Sepoys of the Austrasie Regiment are reported wearing an attractive uniform of green faced black with red trim, while red faced blue was worn by the *Cipayes de l'Îsle de France* (see Plate F). The battalion of *Cipayes de Trinquemalé* (September 1782–late 1783) in Trincomalee, Ceylon, probably wore green with red collar, cuffs and lapels. According to Revel, the historian of the French Sepoys, red was worn by battalions which joined the regiments brought by Bussy in March 1783, with collar, cuffs and lapels of the French regiment's facing colour.

The *Volontaires de Bourbon* (1 April 1779–22 December 1789) had a short coat of white nankeen with green collar, cuffs and lapels, white nankeen waistcoat and gaiter-trousers, white metal buttons, black round hat laced white (see Plate G). The 3rd Company raised 22 December 1782 among free blacks had the same uniform but with blue collar, cuffs and lapels. The *Volontaires indiens* (16 May–1 August 1783) raised among 'the Mistiche nation' in India were assigned a green uniform with red collar, cuffs and lapels, and attached to the *Volontaires de Bourbon*.

Officers and drummers

Officers were to wear the same uniform as their men but made of finer material with gilded or silvered buttons (see Plate G). Rank was distinguished by a complex system of epaulettes in gold or silver, with captains and subalterns having (in scarlet for the metropolitan army, in facing colour for colonial troops) silk lines and diamonds on the straps. The sword knot for all officers was gold, mixed with silk of scarlet for the metropolitan army, facing colour for colonial troops, for captains and subalterns. When on duty, officers wore a gilt gorget with a silver badge bearing the arms of the king at the centre.

Drummers in the French forces wore a livery coat with the regimental facings applied as on the coats of the rest of the regiment and trimmed with livery lace. For the vast majority of regiments this was the blue coat of the king's livery trimmed with the king's livery lace: a white chain on crimson. The lace was to edge the facings, and each coat sleeve was also to be laced 'with seven bands' of the lace set at equal distances (see Plates E & G). There were exceptions to the king's livery: the queen's, the prince's and most foreign regiments. The drummers of La Reine (the queen's) had red coats trimmed with a livery lace of a white chain on blue. The foreign regiments which were 'Royal' such as Royal Deux-Ponts, Royal-Suèdois or Royal Hesse-Darmstadt had the king's livery, but others had their colonel's livery coat colour and lace with the regimental facings. Dillon's Irish regiment had drummers in red with the white-chain-on-crimson lace. Bouillon (German) had white with a white lace edged with black. The drums were of brass and the hoops were of the drummer's coat colour. Drum-majors had the seams of their coat

▲ *Miniature of an officer of the Royal Deux-Ponts regiment, c. 1780, wearing a dark sky-blue coat and collar with yellow lapels, silver buttons and epaulettes as prescribed in the 1779 dress regulations for the army. (Private collection)*

▶ *Chasseur of the Royal Deux-Pont regiment, 1779, wearing light blue with yellow lapels, cuffs and piping, white metal buttons, green epaulettes, hat plume and sabre knot. Note the pre-1776 accoutrement belts shown in all the prints of Isnard's Etat général des uniformes ..., Strasbourg, 1779.*

trimmed with lace and the cuffs edged with silver laces (one in 1776, two in 1779). From 1779, fifers and clarinets had the same uniform as the drummers but without livery lace and with a silver lace edging each cuff.

The drummers of colonial troops went by the same rules and had the king's blue coat with his livery lace. The drummers themselves were blacks in America, Africa and Île-de-France, or natives of India in that country. The drummers of the Îsle-de-France and Pondichery regiments wore a 'cap with a white plume' instead of a hat. The drummers of the *Volontaires de Bourbon* wore the white coat of their unit with two rows of the king's livery lace on the cuffs; the *Chasseurs-royaux de Saint-Domingue* also wore white with a row of the king's livery lace at the cuffs and pockets. Of the foreign units, the drummers and hussar buglers of the *Volontaires étrangers de la Marine* were ordered to wear the king's livery, but the *Volontaires de Nassau* were allowed the orange livery of the Prince of Nassau.

Tropical dress

In the West and East Indies regular French colonial troops wore coats made of lightweight wool with linen lining (and turnbacks), waistcoats, breeches and gaiters. In the East Indies nankeen was used a great deal instead of linen, and it was not yellow in colour but bleached to a 'sparkling white'. The *Volontaires de Bourbon* had their short coats made of nankeen, while the *Chasseurs-royaux de Saint-Domingue* had theirs in linen, and the 1782–1783 Sepoys dressed in cotton or serge.

The metropolitan troops also made allowances for the heat, and we find linen sent to many regiments in the West Indies. This was used certainly for waistcoats and breeches and perhaps for coat linings and even the coats. Von Closen noted that the three regiments from the West Indies at Yorktown 'suffered a great deal from the change of climate . . . since they only had some linen clothing during the siege, when we had some very cold nights'. Of Rochambeau's force, it appears that only the Soissonnois regiment had linen breeches as they marched south in the summer of 1781, a precaution of its colonel which resulted in 'the fewest stragglers and sick of any' French unit. In the East Indies, while at Île-de-France, white nankeen was used to make

Chasseur of the Gatinois regiment, 1779, wearing white with violet lapels and piping, white metal buttons, green epaulettes, hat plume and sabre knot. In 1781, a detachment was with the Spanish at the capture of Pensacola and the regiment was at Yorktown. After Isnard's Etat général des uniformes . . ., *Strasbourg, 1779.*

Chasseur of the Soissonois regiment, 1779, wearing white with crimson lapels, cuffs and piping, yellow metal buttons, green epaulettes, hat plume and sabre knot. The regiment served in the U.S. and was at Yorktown in 1781. After Isnard's Etat général des uniformes . . ., *Strasbourg, 1779.*

coats, waistcoats and breeches for the Royal-Roussillon regiment in August 1782 and also for a detachment of Austrasie in October. In November, woollen clothing sent from France for Royal-Artillerie was deemed useless and exchanged for 'more convenient clothing supplies'. From the above sources, it is obvious the regulation cut and colour was kept except that linen and nankeen replaced wool. The woollen regimental facings may have been simply stitched on the light weight coat if not made of dyed linen or nankeen.

Alliance cockades

During the war, cockades of an allied nation were joined to one's own cockade to symbolise the alliances. The first instance appears to be Rochambeau's order in June 1780 to add black, the cockade colour of the United States, to the white cockade of the French troops landing in the US. Portraits of Spanish colonial officers in Louisiana, c. 1781–1783, show white added to their red Spanish cockades. French troops in the West Indies apparently also added red to their white cockades, as would the French corps serving with the Spanish at Minorca and Gibraltar. It is probable that the Dutch orange cockade was added by the French troops at the Cape, Ceylon, Demerara and the Dutch West Indies. There was also a fashion for triple cockades. The Chevalier de Pontgibaud noted at Corunna, Spain, in 1782 that the Spanish and the French armies wore a white (France), red (Spain) and black (USA) cockade, which also agrees with a self-portrait of Lieutenant de Verger of the Royal Deux-Ponts Regiment.

Conclusion

We asked at the outset if there were other important bodies of French troops apart from Count Rochambeau's corps in the United States. The reader will have seen that the answer is a definite 'yes'. There were, in fact, more important corps of French troops elsewhere in the world, especially the West Indies. The sizeable rôle played by colonial troops (including Sepoys) in those areas has also been taken into account. In terms of material culture studies, the variety of weapons and uniforms—both metropolitan and colonial—is impressive and often exotic. Nor should we end by leaving the impression that only the French and the Americans were fighting

the British. Spain's considerable naval and military contribution has never been properly acknowledged. The Dutch were more timid but held their own. Indeed, the Americans had far more allies fighting the British around the globe than they generally remember nowadays. But most were French; and the independence of the United States owes much to the vast deployment of troops and ships across the world by France between 1778 and 1783.

Bibliography

Louis Suzane, *Histoire de l'infanterie française*, 5 vols. (Paris, 1876) and *Histoire de l'artillerie française* (Paris, 1874); L. Dussieux, *L'armée en France*, vol. 2 (Versailles, 1884); André Corvisier, *Dictionnaire d'art et d'histoire militaire* (Paris, 1988); *The American Campaigns of Rochambeau's Army*, ed. by Howard R. Rice and Anne S. K. Brown (Princeton & Providence, 1972); Vicomte de Noïalles, *Marins et soldats français en Amérique pendant la guerre de l'indépendance des Etats-Unis, 1778–1783* (Paris,

Chasseur of the Touraine regiment, 1779, wearing white with pink cuffs and piping, white metal buttons, green epaulettes, hat plume and sabre knot. The regiment served in the West Indies and at Yorktown. After Isnard's Etat général des uniformes..., *Strasbourg, 1779.*

1903); E. Rufz, *Etudes Historiques et statistiques sur la population de la Martinique* (Saint-Pierre, Martinique, 1850); S. P. Sen, *The French in India, 1763–1816* (Calcutta, 1958); G. B. Malleson, *Final French Struggles in India and on the Indian Seas* (London, 1878); *Journal de Bussy*, ed. by A. Martineau (Paris, 1932); Jonathan R. Dull, *The French Navy and American Independence* (Princeton, 1975); Michel Pétard. *Equipements militaires*, vol. 2. (Saint-Julien-de-Concelles, 1985); Jean Boudriot, *Armes à feu françaises, modèles d'ordonnance*, cahiers 5 & 6 (Paris, 1961 & 1963); Christian Ariès, *Armes blanches militaires françaises* (1967–1988); Pierre Nardin, *Gribeauval, Lieutenant général des armées du roi*

1715–1789 (Paris, 1982). The *Etat Militaire de France* from 1776 to 1783 and the weekly *Gazette de France* from 1778 to 1783 are invaluable contemporary publications. At the *Archives Nationales* in Paris, we have consulted the Marine series A1, vols. 123 to 132, and Colonies series A and F3, for orders pertaining to the colonial troops and marines; Colonies C8A (Martinique) vols. 77 to 84; C9A (Saint-Domingue) vols. 147 to 151; D2C for various returns. At the *Service historique de l'armée de terre* in Vincennes, *Archives de la Guerre*, series A1, vols. 3704 to 3731; Xi, boxes 1 to 3; *Ordonnances* (by date) as well as the photostats of regimental records at the Library of Congress in Washington.

THE PLATES

A1: Volontaire, Cadets de Saint-Pierre, 1778

This Martinique volunteer unit of six officers and 103 ORs is recorded taking part in the capture of Dominica by the French. The uniform was a blue coat with yellow cuffs and grey turnbacks, the coat and cuffs edged with a third-of-an-inch silver lace for enlisted volunteers and two-thirds of an inch for officers; nankeen waistcoat and breeches; hat laced with black velvet and a white plume. The volunteers were allowed the unfringed epaulette of sub-lieutenants, which was of yellow silk with silver lace diamonds. The officers had similar epaulettes to those of the regulars. (Arch. Nat., Colonies, F3, v. 262)

Officer of the Armagnac infantry regiment wearing the uniform prescribed by the February 1799 regulation: white coat with sky-blue lapels and piping at the cuffs and pocket flaps, silver buttons and epaulettes. The regiment first received 466 uniforms of this pattern in early 1781 but 934 soldiers had received no issues of any kind since 18 to 24 months and were allowed at Guadeloupe locally produced cloth "ample" waistcoats and linen trousers in July 1781. It appears that the regiment was finally re-clothed by May 1782. This regiment saw a considerable amount of action in the West Indies and also supplied detachments at the siege of Savannah in 1799, at Demerara and for La Pérouse's expedition in Hudson's Bay in Canada during 1782. Watercolour by G. A. Embleton. (Canadian Parks Service)

A2: Chasseur, Régiment de Viennois, 1778

A soldier as he might have appeared at the attack on Dominica. The uniform shown is in strict accordance with the 1776 regulation described, although it appears that bugle horns on the turnbacks and green epaulettes were already becoming popular among the newly created Chasseur companies. (*Règlement arrêté par le roi concernant l'habillement et l'équipement de ses troupes. Du 31 mai 1776*, Paris, 1776; M. Pétard, 'L'homme de 1776, le fusilier', *Uniformes*, No. 56, 1980)

A3: Officer, Martinique Militia, Fort-Royal Battalion, c. 1778–1780

The militia from the French islands supported the regular troops in the early campaigns, such as the capture of Dominica led by the daring Governor-General of Martinique, the Marquis de Bouillé. Since the 1760s the Martinique and St. Lucia militias had had a blue uniform with gold buttons and hat lace. The colour of the cuffs distinguished the various battalions, and our officer—who was more likely to have a uniform—has the white cuffs of the Fort-Royal battalion; the Saint-Pierre battalion had red cuffs, Mouillage had yellow, Trinité had black, Basse-Pointe had pink, etc. Militias in Guadeloupe and Guyana usually had white with various facings, while those of Saint-Domingue—now Haiti—wore many colours. (M. Durand-Molard, *Code de la Martinique*, St. Pierre, Martinique, 1807, v. 2)

B1: Grenadier, Martinique Regiment, 1778–1783

Colonial regiments had their own uniform regulations, different from those of the metropolitan army. In the West Indies and French Guyana blue single-breasted coats with collars and cuffs of the facing colour—buff in the case of Martinique—were worn. Grenadiers were distinguished by epaulettes of the facing colour and a short sabre. (Arch. Nat., AD VII, carton 3)

B2: Fusilier, Dillon's (Irish) Regiment, 1779

According to a contemporary watercolour of the French assault on Grenada by a Swiss observer, Dillon's wore a mixture consisting of the 1776 coat and gaiters with pre-1776 type of hat and waistcoat, and accoutrements. It was a time of transition and, no doubt, many units displayed such variety, especially with regards to accoutrements, which did not wear out as quickly as uniforms. (Paul Morand, *Monsieur Dumoulin à l'Îsle de la Grenade*, Paudex, Switzerland, 1976)

This drummer of the Auxerrois regiment is typical of the uniform prescribed to these battlefield musicians in the French army. He wears the blue coat of the royal livery trimmed with the royal livery lace as did the great majority of units, and has the 1779 regimental distinctions: black lapels and white metal buttons. Drummers were "armed" with a brass drum and carried a hanger. This regiment saw much action in the West Indies, supplied detachments at the siege of Savannah in 1779 and for La Pérouse's expedition in Hudson's Bay in Canada during 1782. Watercolour by G. A. Embleton. (Canadian Parks Service)

B3: Volunteer, Chasseurs-volontaires de Saint-Domingue, 1779

This was the first unit of full-time serving free black troops to be sent into action in the annals of the French forces. The siege of Savannah was a failure, but the black troops earned distinction by successfully covering the re-embarkation of the French army. Part of the corps was disbanded, but a detachment of 148 men arrived on the island of Grenada on 1 December 1779 and was reported still there in August 1782. A 20-man detachment is also reported serving as marines on board *Le Citoyen* during 1780. (Moreau de Saint-Méry, *Loix et constitutions de colonies française de l'Amérique sous le vent*, Paris, 1786–1790, v. 5)

C1: Hussar, Volontaires étrangers de la Marine, 1778–1783

Up to eight legions of these mostly German-speaking volunteers were planned to be raised by the ministry of the navy for service overseas; three came into existence. The 1st Legion served in the West Indies from 1779 until disbanded (except for the hussars) in late 1782; the 2nd was transformed into Lauzun's

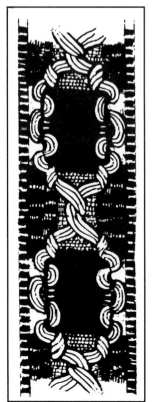

◀ *Pattern of the King's livery lace. (Francis Back)*

▶ Compagnie franche de Saint-Pierre-et-Miquelon *fusilier wearing the uniform in use from 1766 to 1778. It consisted of a blue coat with blue cuffs, red lapels and collar, white turnbacks and white metal buttons stamped with an anchor design as with all French marine and colonial troops. White waistcoat, breeches, gaiters and cravat; black hat laced white; white leather accoutrements with black cartridge box and bayonet scabbard. The .69 calibre musket is a Model 1763. Watercolour by Michel Pétard. (Canadian Parks Service)*

Legion and sent to the United States in 1780; the 3rd served in India during 1782–1783. Each legion had two companies of hussars which went overseas; those of the 3rd are reported in Île-de-France and India, and those of the 1st in the West Indies. A detachment of the hussars of the 1st Legion was part of the troops sent up from the West Indies at the siege of Yorktown. The hussars of the legions wore sky-blue dolmans with yellow breeches and white braid.

(Arch. Nat., Marine, A1, 123; *The Revolutionary Journal of Baron Ludwig Von Closen 1780–1783*, ed. E. M. Acomb, 1958)

C2: Gunner, Royal-Artillerie 1779–1783

This man is wearing the regulation 1779 uniform. Note the short sword with an eagle-headed 'Roman' grip introduced from 1771. (*La Sabretache*, 1896, 1976, 1977)

At the left, a Canonnier-bombardier *N.C.O. of the colonial artillery companies in India, c. 1776–78. The uniform was blue with red collar and cuffs, blue turnbacks, yellow shoulder strap, brass buttons, white waistcoat, breeches and gaiters, hat laced with yellow tape. The uniform of the West Indian companies of* Canonniers-bombardiers *was identical except for red turnbacks and an aurore shoulder strap. Gunners in the colonies were classed elite troops and wore the brass-hilted M. 1767 army hanger and could have the moustache as they were considered grenadiers when not performing artillery duties. The figure to the right is a Cipaye de l'Inde from the Sepoy battalion formed in 1773 and which served gallently at the defence of Pondichery in 1778. The battalion's uniform was a short blue coat with yellow collar, cuffs and lapels, white turnbacks, white metal buttons, white waistcoat, white Indian breeches trimmed with blue and a white turban. Although not quite regulation, our man also sports an Indian "Talwar" sword which appears to have been "tolerated" for some Sepoys. Watercolour by Michel Pétard. (Canadian Parks Service)*

C3: Infantry private, 1st Legion, Volontaire étrangers de la Marine, 1778–1782

The infantry uniform prescribed on 1 September 1778 for the corps was sky-blue, the colour of German regiments in the French forces, with yellow collar for the 1st Legion. (Arch. Nat., Marine, A1, 123)

D1: Hussar, Lauzun's Legion, USA, 1780–1783

Three hundred hussars were sent to the US; half of them were issued lances, so that they were sometimes called 'Lauzun's Lancers'. They wore sky-blue dolmans with yellow braid, and a veteran of Yorktown remembered them wearing 'blue roundabouts & yellow edging'. They also had scarlet breeches laced yellow. They left France with their pelisses in 1780, but Lauzun reported in 1783 that they had

◀ *Fusilier of the Port-au-Prince colonial infantry regiment c. 1776–86. A detachment served at the sieges of Savannah (1779). The blue coat was trimmed with the regiment's red collar, cuffs and shoulder straps edged with white piping and had white metal buttons. The colonial infantry had hats laced white and this uniform remained unchanged until 1786. (Anne S. K. Brown Military Collection, Brown University, Providence, USA)*

▲ *Fusilier of the Martinique colonial infantry regiment c. 1776–86. This regiment saw much action in the West Indies and also had detachments serving at Savannah (1779) and Pensacola (1781). The blue coat was trimmed with the regiment's buff collar, cuffs and shoulder straps edged with white piping and had white metal buttons. The colonial infantry had hats laced white and this uniform remained unchanged until 1784. (Anne S. K. Brown Military Collection, Brown University, Providence, USA)* none left, and did not replace them due to the heat in Virginia. Americans also reported that the hussars wore moustaches. (Pension declaration of Thomas Madeira, US National Archives; Arch. Guerre, *Ordonnances*, 5 March 1780)

D2: Gunner, Royal-Artillerie, c. 1780–1783

When serving the guns, the personnel of the artillery would usually wear their blue *pokalem* forage caps with a red lily and red edging to the front flap, blue waistcoat with red cuffs (but blue collar), and blue breeches. (*La Sabretache*, 1896, 1976, 1977)

D3: Infantry corporal, Lauzun's Legion, USA, 1780–1782

It is often overlooked that half of Lauzun's 600 men consisted of infantry. The uniform was sky-blue with yellow lapels and cuffs, white collar and epaulettes and white metal buttons. The rank of corporal is shown by the two laces on the lower sleeve and the short sabre. (Arch. Guerre, *Ordonnances*, 5 March 1780)

E1: Grenadier, Bourbonnois Regiment, USA, 1780–1782

The grenadiers were noted in Philadelphia wearing bearskin caps, an item theoretically not worn since 1776. Many grenadiers ignored this order and Bourbonnois may not have been the only unit smuggling the proud grenadier's headgear overseas. (Closen's *Journal*)

E2: Drummer, Royal Deux-Ponts (German) Regiment, USA, 1780–1782

The drummers of this regiment wore the king's livery with regimental facings, since it was 'royal'—unlike most foreign units, which had their music dressed in the colonel's livery. (Streidbeck's MS, Musée d'Alsace; *Règlement . . . 1779*)

E3: Fusilier, Saintonge Regiment, USA, 1780–1781

Our man is one of about 200 recorded as still wearing the 1776 coat at Yorktown, with aurore cuffs and lapels and sky-blue collar. (*Règlement . . . 1776*; Pension declaration of Thomas Madeira, US National Archives; Library of Congress, Saintonge Regt. record copies)

Fusilier of the Guadeloupe colonial infantry regiment c. 1776–86. Detachments served at St. Lucia (1778) and Savannah (1779). The blue coat was trimmed with the regiment's crimson collar, cuffs and shoulder strap edged with white piping and had white metal buttons. The colonial infantry had hats laced white and this uniform remained unchanged until 1784. (Anne S. K. Brown Military Collection, Brown University, Providence, USA)

E4: Chasseur, Saintonge Regiment, USA, 1780–1782

This contrasting figure wears the 1779 uniform with the distinctions of chasseurs: green epaulettes and bugle horns on the turnbacks. (*Règlement ... 1779*)

F1: Sepoy, Île-de-France Regiment, India, 1782–1783

Red with blue collar, cuffs and lapels worn by the *Cipayes de l'Île de France*. This uniform was somewhat the same as the British Sepoys, but red seems to have been popular with Sepoys serving many nations and princes at this time. The French stipulated only green uniforms from 1786 to avoid confusion. (Arch. Nat., Colonies, D2C, 192)

F2: Fusilier, Île-de-France Regiment, India, 1782–1783

At least three battalions of this four-battalion colonial regiment served in India, some detached to Hyder-Ali's Mysorian army as far as the Malabar coast. (Arch. Nat., Colonies, A, 109)

F3: Sepoy, Austrasie Regiment, India, 1782–1783

An officer of Austrasie described in March 1782 the dress of the two battalions of *Cipayes d'Austrasie* as green short coat with black cuffs and lapels, short white waistcoat, green short trousers, red sash, and green turban decorated with red, adding that this uniform 'looked very good'. (*Memoires du Chevalier de Mautort*, ed. Baron Clermont-Tonnerre, 1895)

G1: Fusilier, Volontaires de Bourbon, 1779–1783

The corps was renowned for the very accurate shooting of its men, many of whom were expert hunters since childhood in the hills of their island home of Île-de-Bourbon. They had a ventral cartrid-

Fusilier of the Du Cap colonial infantry regiment c. 1776–86. Detachments served at the sieges of Savannah (1779) and Pensacola (1781). The blue coat was trimmed with the regiment's saxon green collar, cuffs and shoulder straps edged with white piping and had white metal buttons. The colonial infantry had hats laced white and this uniform remained unchanged until 1786. (Anne S. K. Brown Military Collection, Brown University, Providence, USA)

ge box holding 20 rounds and a horn holding a pound and a half of powder rather than the standard equipment. (Arch. Nat., Colonies, D2C, 41; *Journal de Bussy*, 22 Dec. 1782)

G2: Drummer, La Mark (German) Regiment, India, 1783

This regiment had drummers and bandsmen dressed in the colonel's livery. For drummers, this consisted of a white coat with the regimental facings and a black and white checkered lace—in India, some locals were enlisted. Bandsmen had the same uniform but without livery lace. (*Le Passepoil*, 1934; Streidbeck's MS, Musée d'Alsace)

G3: Officer, Aquitaine Regiment, India, 1783

For service in the field company officers were armed with light muskets and cartridge boxes as well as their swords, and each was equipped with a cartridge box holding 16 rounds with a white belt. Our officer wears the cross of the Royal and Military Order of Saint-Louis hung on a scarlet ribbon, a decoration instituted by Louis XIV in 1693 for officers giving distinguished service. (*Règlement ... 1779*)

H1: Officer, French Navy, 1778–1783

French naval officers had a superb full dress of dark blue faced with scarlet, laced elaborately with gold, for formal occasions. Most of the time, and especially at sea, they wore a plain undress uniform consisting of a dark blue frock with gold buttons and epaulettes, scarlet waistcoat, breeches and stockings, and a gold-laced hat. (M. Pétard, 'L'uniforme des officiers de Marine', *Uniformes*, No. 65, 1982)

H2: Bombardier, Bombardiers de la Marine, 1778–1783

This gunner is wearing the corps uniform complete

Fusilier of the Îsle-de-France colonial infantry regiment c. 1776–86 wearing the white uniform with blue facings and white metal buttons, hat laced white, a dress which did not change until 1786. From 1782, this four-battalion regiment saw considerable – and largely still unknown – service in southern India. Part of the regiment was on the Coromandel coast but another part was with Typoo Sultan's forces on the Malabor coast. (Anne S. K. Brown Military Collection, Brown University, Providence, USA)

with the bearskin cap and short sabre indicating an élite unit. There was also a working dress consisting of a blue fatigue cap piped red, a blue jacket faced red, and white sailor's trousers. (J. Boudriot, *The 74 Gun Ship*, vol. 4)

H3: Fusilier, Corps royal de l'infanterie de la Marine, 1778–1783

From 1774 the 12,000 French marines wore this blue uniform faced red and a working dress similar to the Bombardiers. In 1782 a few minor modifications to the uniform were ordered made, such as scarlet piping to the waistcoats, but it is doubtful that the changes were actually made before the end of hostilities. (J. Boudriot, *The 74 Gun Ship*, vol. 4)

H4: Fusilier, Barrois Regiment, 1776–1782

This regiment did not serve overseas but contributed detachments to serve on board warships as marines. Our fusilier is from a detachment on board the frigate *La Cléopâtre*, which wore the 1776 *redingote* until August 1782 when replaced with linen clothing at Île-de-France. This ample garment was white with the regimental orange collar, blue cuffs and piping, and white metal buttons. The *redingote* would have been worn as a working garment with a *pokalem* and sailor's trousers. (*Journal de Bussy*, 8 August 1782; *Règlement 1776*)

▲ *Fusilier of the Pondichery colonial infantry regiment c. 1776–78 wearing the white uniform with orange facings and white metal buttons in use at the time of the siege of Pondichery in 1778. There, in a hopeless situation, the regiment fought with great distinction. At the surrender, the British granted the honour of war and allowed the unit to keep its colours. (Anne S. K. Brown Military Collection, Brown University, Providence, USA)*

◀ *Reversed print showing a back view of a hussar of the 2nd Legion of the Volontaires étrangers de la Marine, 1778–80. This unique print shows details not mentioned in the corps uniform instruction of 30 September 1778: the plume at the cap, the numeral "2" on the cartridge box and the hearts at the elbows. Note also the anchor design on the sabretache.*

In 1780, the 2nd Legion became a distinct unit under the command of the Duke of Lauzun and won lasting fame as "Lauzun's Legion" in the United States where it served from 1780 to 1783. Photo by Raoul Brunon. (Bibliothèque Raoul & Jean Brunon, Musée de l'Armée. Château de l'Empéri, Salon-de-Provence, France)

Notes sur les planches en couleur

A1 Une unité ayant la force d'une compagnie prit part à la capture française de la Dominique. Les volontaires portaient cet uniforme, avec épaulettes sans franges; pour les officiers, la manchette à dentelle et le liseré sur le manteau étaient deux fois plus larges, avec épaulettes réglementaires d'officiers. **A2** L'uniforme réglementaire de 1776, bien que les ornementations sur les retroussis en forme de cor de chasse et les épaulettes vertes aient déjà grande vogue parmi les nouvelles compagnies de Chasseurs. **A3** La milice de Sainte Lucie portait déjà cet uniforme. La couleur des revers de manche distinguait les bataillons, ici le blanc pour Fort-Royal.

B1 Une ordonnance spéciale existait déjà pour l'uniforme des régiments coloniaux, qui différait de celui des régiments de la métropole. Le col et les revers de manche en buffle distinguait le régiment de la Martinique, et la couleur du parement sur le revers de manche était répétée dans les épaulettes des grenadiers. Toutes les unités des Antilles et de la Guyane portaient des manteaux droits, bleus. **B2** Une aquarelle de l'époque montre cet uniforme porté par les soldats irlandais du régiment de Dillon à Grenade, 1779 – le manteau de 1776 et les guêtres, un chapeau plus ancien, un gilet et le fourniment. **B3** La première unité à temps complet de noirs libres dans l'histoire des forces françaises servit au siège de Savannah en 1779, sur l'île de Grenade en 1779–82, et un détachement servit à bord du navire *Le Citoyen* en tant que fusiliers marins, 1780.

C1 Chacune des trois légions vraiment formées avaient deux compagnies de hussards, ces derniers portaient tous cet uniforme de base. **C2** Uniforme réglementaire de 1779; notez l'épée de 1771 avec pommeau à tête d'aigle. **C3** Les cols jaunes identifiaient la 1ère Légion conformément aux réglementations de septembre 1778 pour l'uniforme de l'infanterie.

D1 Quelque 300 hussards – la moitié d'entre eux armés de lances – furent envoyés en Amérique. Ils avaient, à l'origine, des pelisses, mais ces dernières ne furent pas remplacées quand elles furent usées en service. **D2** Uniforme caractéristique pour les travaux difficiles avec les canons, y compris le pokalem, un bonnet de police, et le gilet bleu avec revers de manche rouges. **D3** L'un des fantassins de l'infanterie de Lauzun, souvent oubliée; le rang est indiqué par les deux raies de dentelle sur l'avant-bras.

E1 On vit certainement des bonnets en peau d'ours en Philadelphie, bien qu'ils ne fussent plus réglementaires depuis 1776. **E2** Régiment "royal", ce qui était peu courant parmi les unités étrangères, ses tambours portant la livrée du roi. **E3** On enregistra 200 hommes environ de cette unité portent toujours l'uniforme de 1776 à Yorktown. **E4** Par contraste, ce soldat porte l'uniforme de 1779, avec distinctions de Chasseur.

F1 De nombreuses unités sepoy portaient fondamentalement des uniformes rouges; la couleur changea à verte à partir de 1786, pour éviter la confusion avec les sepoys britanniques à manteau rouge. **F2** Trois des quatre bataillons de ce régiment servirent en Inde. **F3** Un officier du régiment a décrit cet uniforme, porté par les deux bataillons de sepoy détachés auprès du Régt. Austrasie.

G1 Ces tireurs d'élite, recrutés parmi les chasseurs de l'Île de Bourbon, avaient une poche à munitions ventrale, pour 20 caratouches et un cornet à poudre séparé. **G2** Certaines autochtones furent enrôlés pendant le service en Inde. Les tambars portaient la livrée de colonel; notez la garniture en dentelle noire et blanches sur le manteau. **G3** Pour le service en campagne, les officiers portaient des mousquets légers et des poches à cartouches. Cet officier est décoré de l'Ordre Militaire et Royal de St. Louis sur ruban écarlate.

H1 Les officiers de la Marine avaient un bel uniforme de grande tenue bleu foncé avec parements rouges et galons dorés; mais en mer, ils portaient surtout un uniforme de petite tenue, bleu uni, avec boutons et épaulettes dorés, gilet écarlate, culottes et bas. **H2** A part cette grande tenue, il y avait un uniforme de travail avec bonnet bleu au liseré rouge, veste bleue à parement rouge et pantalons blancs de marins. **H3** Cet uniforme a été introduit en 1774; également tenue de travail similaire à celle des Bombardiers. **H4** Servant à bord de la frégate *La Cléopâtre*, il porte la redingote de 1776; il aurait portée en tenue de travail avec le pokalem et les pantalons de marin.

Farbtafeln

A1 Eine Einheit in Kompanie-Stärke war an der französichen Einnahme von Dominica beteiligt. Diese Uniform mit fransenlosen Epauletten wurde von Freiwilligen getragen; Offiziere hatten Spitzenbesatz an Manschetten und Mantel, der zweimal so breit war, und dazu die regulären Offizierspauletten. **A2** Die Standarduniform von 1776, wenn auch bei den neuen Chasseur-Kompanien bereits Trompeten-Ornemente und grüne Epauletten populär waren. **A3** Diese Uniform wurde auch von der Miliz von St. Lucia getragen. Manschettenfarmen identifizierten die Bataillone – hier weiß für Port-Royal.

B1 Kolonialregimenter hatten eigene Uniformvorschriften als die Metropolitan-Regimenter. Sandfarbene Kragen und Manschetten kennzeichneten das Regiment von Martinique, und diese Aufschlagfarbe fand sich auch in den Grenadier-Epauletten. Alle Einheiten aus Westindien und Guyana trugen blaue, einreihige Mäntel. **B2** Ein zeitgenössisches Aquarell zeigt diese Uniforme der Iren in Dillons Regiment in Grenada im Jahre 1779 – der Mantel und die Gamaschen sind von 1776, die Mütze, Weste und Zubehör sing älter. **B3** Die erste ständige Einheit von freien Schwarzen in der Geschichte der französischen Armee war bei der Belagerung von Savannah 1779 im Einsatz, dann in Grenada 1779–82, und eine Abteilung diente auch als Marinesoldaten an Bord de Le Citoyen im Jahre 1780.

C1 Jede der drei tatsächlich gebildeten Legionen hatte zwei Husarenkompanien, die alle diese Grunduniform trugen. **C2** Standarduniform von 1779; siehe Säbel von 1771 mit Adlerkopfknauf. **C3** Gelbe Kragen kennzeichneten die 1. Legion entsprechend der Uniformvorschriften vom September 1778.

D1 Rund 300 Husaren – die Hälfte davon mit Lanzen bewaffnet – wurden nach Amerika geschickt. Sie hatten ursprünglich imhänge, die aber nach ihrer Abnutzung im Dienst nich erneuert wurden. **D2** Typisch Uniform für den schweren Dienst an Kanonen, einschließlich des Pokalem-Käppis und der blauen Weste mit roten Manschetten. **D3** Ein Mann aus der oft vergessenen Infanterie von Lauzon; sein Rang wird durch die beiden Litzen aum Unterarm angezeigt.

E1 Bärenmützen konnte man zweifellos in Philadelphia sehen, obwohl sie seit 1776 nicht mehr vorschriftsmäßig waren. **E2** Dieses Regiment war "königlich", was unter fremden Einheiten ungewöhnlich war, und die Trommler trugen königliche Uniformen. **E3** Etwa 200 Mann der Einheit trugen bei Yorktown immer noch die Uniform von 1776. **E4** Im Gegensatz dazu trägt dieser Mann eine Uniform von 1779 mit den Chasseur-Distinktionen.

F1 Viele Sepoy-Einheiten trugen hauptsächlich rote Uniformen; ab 1786 wurden diese Uniformen grün, um Verwechslungen mit den rotröckigen britischen Sepoys zu vermeiden. **F2** Drei der vier Bataillone des Regiments dienten in Indien. **F3** Ein Offizier des Regiments beschrieb diese Uniform der beiden Sepoy-Bataillone des Regiments Austrasie.

G1 Diese Scharfschützen, angeworben aus den Jägern der Isle de Bourbonhatten einen Gürtel für 20 Patronen und ein separates Pulverhorn. **G2** Manche Ortsansässige wurden in Indien während des dortigen Einsatzes angeworben. Die Trommler trugen die Farben des Obersten; siehe schwarzweißen Litzenbesatz am Mantel. **G3** Im Feldeinsatz trugen die Offiziere leichte Musken und Patronengurten. Dieser Offizier trägt den Royal and Military Order von St. Louis an einem schlarlachroten Band.

H1 Marineoffiziere hatten eine vornehme Galauniform in Dukelblau mit roten Aufschlägen und Goldlitzen; auf See aber trugen sie meistens eine einfache blaue Dienstuniform mit Goldknöpfen und Epauletten, schlarlachrote Weste, Breeches und Kniestrümpfe. **H2** Abgesehen von dieser Galauniform gab es Dienstuniformen mit blauem, rot eingefaßtem Käppi, eine blaue, roteingefaßte Jacke und weiße Matrosenhose. **H3** 1774 eingeführte Uniform; es gab auch Arbeitskleidung ähnlich jener der Bombardiere. **H4** Er diente an Bord der Frigatte La Cléopâtre und trägt das Redingote von 1776; für den Alltag würde es mit dem Pokalem und mit Matrosenhose getragen werden.